D0402077

For Joyce, Barbara, Terry, and Rich—with my thanks!

For Toby, Len, and Meredith Friedman, who opened their Berkshire home to a struggling music teacher turned Spooky author.

For my family: David, Dena, Tim, Arlene, Hannah, Emma, Nathan, Ben, Deb, Gabe, Clare, Jack, Chris, Karen, Davey, and Millie.

* * *

Contents

SPOOKY
Massachusetts

*Tales of Hauntings, Strange Happenings,
and Other Local Lore*

RETOLD BY S. E. SCHLOSSER

ILLUSTRATED BY PAUL G. HOFFMAN

Guilford, Connecticut

Map by Lisa Reneson © Rowman & Littlefield
Illustrations and map border by Paul G. Hoffman

Library of Congress Cataloging-in-Publication Data

Schlosser, S. E.
    Spooky Massachusetts : tales of hauntings, strange happenings, and other
local lore/retold by S. E. Schlosser; illustrations by Paul G. Hoffman.
        p. cm.
    ISBN-13: 978-0-7627-4852-5
    1. Ghosts—Massachusetts. 2. Occultism—Massachusetts. I. Hoffman, Paul
G. II. Title.
    BF1472.U6S32   2008
    398.209744—dc22

                                                        2008016207

ISBN 978-0-7627-4852-5

Printed in the United States of America

Distributed by NATIONAL BOOK NETWORK

PART TWO: POWERS OF DARKNESS AND LIGHT

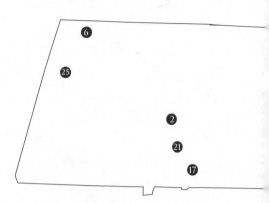

Introduction

I've spent a great deal of time in the Bay State: summer vacations in Cape Cod and the Berkshires, business trips to Boston, and long weekends spent at the home of my college roommate, who lived just outside Worcester. Whenever I visit, I am always struck by the beauty of the landscape. From the Berkshire Hills to the Atlantic Ocean, Massachusetts is an amazingly lovely state. But more impressive to me are the people who inhabit her. Practical, kind, good-natured, hard-working, and fun to be with, the people of the Bay State always give me a warm welcome. Perhaps the word that sums them up best is "plucky."

Indeed, Massachusetts has always been filled with that wonderful contrariness that we call "high spirits" or "pluck." The state began as a land full of peaceful—and not so peaceful—Native American tribes, who fished, hunted, and planted corn; who loved and married (*The Missing Bride*); and who lived and died upon these shores. These same Native Americans welcomed first the Norsemen, then the explorers, and finally the Pilgrims and Puritans to this land.

And, speaking of the Pilgrims, how about the pluck

they showed in coming to Massachusetts so they could freely practice their religion? Little did they know when they stepped ashore on Plymouth Rock that survival in this harsh new world would force them to adapt their customs and thinking so much that they would found a whole new breed of plucky people that we call "Yankees."

The Pilgrims were quickly followed by the Puritans, who brought to this land their strict religious beliefs and who—for a time—engaged in a ferocious witch-hunt that convulsed the entire colony (*Madness*). Nowhere was there a pluckier—and unluckier—man at that time than Giles Corey, who suffered a torturous death rather than allow the colony to take his property away from his heirs.

Never did the pluck and contrariness and sheer patriotism of the Bay State shine through more clearly than during the events leading up to the American Revolution (*Dark Portrait*). And of course, the "shot heard 'round the world" was discharged in the Massachusetts Bay Province (*Time Warp*).

One of the most moving folktales I have ever heard also comes from Massachusetts and involves a "little washer woman"—an Irishwoman's ghost who returns to the stream near her home after dying in childbirth to wash and wash her dead child's garments (*Bean-Nighe*). In life, the Irishwoman in this tale was a member of another plucky group that was quite active in Massachusetts—the abolitionists—and her family carries on this work after she is gone.

The Bay State is so full of plucky individuals and the wonderful folklore they have created that I could ramble on for days and barely touch the surface. Massachusetts lore features characters like Peter Rugg, who is still trying to make it back to Boston after more than 200 years of searching for the road home (*Which Way to Boston?*); the Nantucket whaling captain who sees a ghost aboard his ship (*Thar She Blows!*); and Sam Hart, who raced his horse against the Devil (*The Black Horse*), all of whose tales are retold in this collection. I invite you to read about these plucky folks, and when you're through, perhaps you'll tell me your own tales of Massachusetts. I'm all ears!

—Sandy Schlosser

PART ONE
Ghost Stories

Death Omen

NEW BEDFORD

I turned left out of my business parking lot on Friday evening instead of right, heading toward the highway. I was making the three-hour trip to my friend Sarah's house, where I planned to spend the weekend. Sarah was recently divorced and appreciated company whenever she could get it. Since my husband was away on a business trip, I had called Sarah and invited myself to her place. She was delighted to accept my spur-of-the-moment invitation.

As I traveled down the dark, wet highway, I kept feeling chills, as though something bad were going to happen or someone were watching me. I kept looking in the rearview mirror and glancing into the back seat. No one was there. *Don't be ridiculous,* I told myself, wishing fervently that I was home in my bed instead of driving on a dark, rainy highway. There was almost no traffic on the road, so I kept going, knowing that I would soon reach New Bedford.

I turned off the highway and started traveling down the local roads that led to Sarah's house. At exactly 9:52 p.m. according to the clock on my dashboard, I drew alongside the town cemetery. As I drove down the street, I saw a strange light glowing among the tombstones. Curious, I stopped the car to take a look, and I saw a figure moving—a glowing female figure, walking slowly, as if she carried a heavy weight. *A ghost,* I thought in alarm.

As I sat frozen, my car idling, the ghost seemed to hear the sound of the engine, and she looked up. I gasped in fear. She had the twisted face of a demon, with glowing red eyes and short pointed teeth. I screamed as she leapt toward the car, her clawed hands reaching toward me. I slammed my foot down on the accelerator and the car leapt forward. For a few terrible moments, she ran among the tombstones, keeping pace with the car. Then she fell behind.

In the rearview mirror, I saw the ghost grow taller and taller, until she was as large as a tree. Red light swirled around her like mist. She pointed after me, her mouth moving, though I could not make out her words. I jerked my attention back to the road, afraid what might happen if I let my car run off the street.

I made it to Sarah's house in record time and flung myself out of the car, pounding on her door frantically and looking behind me to see if the demon-faced woman had followed me. Sarah came running to the door and let me in. I ran past her into the safety of the house and fell with a gasp into a chair.

"Jane, what's wrong?" Sarah asked, shutting the door behind me and sinking down into the chair next to mine.

I couldn't speak for a few moments. There was a huge knot in my chest that grew so tight I gasped for breath whenever I pictured the face of the woman in the cemetery. Sarah was going to think I had lost my mind, but I had to tell someone what had happened or the knot in my chest would strangle

DEATH OMEN

me. After several false starts, I managed to choke out my story. Sarah gasped and asked, "The phantom? Was it walking in the cemetery when you saw it?"

I nodded, puzzled by her question.

"It must have been the witch," Sarah said, wringing her hands.

"The witch?" I asked.

"They say that the ghost of an accused witch haunts the cemetery," Sarah said. "She's considered a death omen. People see her when something terrible is about to happen to them or someone they know."

Ordinarily, I would have laughed at such a superstition, but the appearance of the phantom had shaken me.

After a few minutes' conversation and a cup of hot cocoa, I felt calm enough to retrieve my luggage from the car, though I foolishly begged Sarah to come with me, since the thought of facing the darkness alone made my hands shake. As it was, I froze on the doorstep, the red eyes and crazed face of the witch's ghost looming in my mind until Sarah gave me an impatient push from behind. Then I hurried down the steps and unlocked the sedan. Moments later, we were back inside, laughing a little at my fear and haste. Sarah sat on the edge of the bed as I unpacked my few things, eagerly outlining the events she had planned for the weekend.

It was nearly midnight when the front doorbell rang. Sarah and I stared at each other in surprise. Who could be coming to the door at this time of night? Before my eyes flashed once again the leering form of the phantom witch, said to appear just before a disaster. My hands started to shake so much that I dropped the hairbrush I was holding. Sarah swallowed and then shook her head. "You said it yourself," she said, in a far-too-calm voice, "It was just superstitious nonsense."

Tossing her head bravely, she marched out of the room and down the stairs. I trailed behind her and stood on the bottom step as she opened the door to find the tall figure of a policeman. The look on his face was a mixture of pained duty and compassion; his words brief and to the point. Sarah's parents had been involved in a car accident that evening and had both been killed instantly. The time of death? 9:52 p.m.

2

Which Way to Boston?

NORTHAMPTON

It had been a day of "Ds," Peter mused to himself as he turned his car onto the twisty, tree-lined, isolated side road he used as a shortcut whenever he was late driving home. Dreary, dark, and drizzling were the first three that came to mind.

"A dreary, dark, and drizzling dusk," Peter said aloud, liking the way the words rolled off his tongue. He peered through the swishing windshield wipers that were swiping ineffectively at the raindrops dotting his windshield. The wipers seemed to be creating a nasty smudge on the passenger side of the car, he noticed with a wry smile. Of course. Didn't they always?

His headlights barely pierced the gloomy avenue as he drove through the dimming daylight. Suddenly, his engine started to knock—one, two, three times—and then stalled abruptly. A bright orange warning light flared on his dashboard, and Peter almost said another "D" word but hastily bit back the curse. His wife, Mandy, was trying to break him of his habitual swearing.

"You're as bad as the other Peter Rugg," Mandy had told him the previous week, shaking her finger at him in mock anger as she referenced his historical namesake.

The first Peter Rugg was a famous character in an old Boston folktale. According to the legend, Peter Rugg was an upright Boston colonist whose prim and proper manner was often overwhelmed by his terrible temper. Once aroused, Peter Rugg was famous for his ability to swear the paint off a wall and his fondness for kicking down doors, dashing about in circles, and yelling so loud that his wig flipped over. Even the bravest of men fled before his wrath. It was this terrible habit of swearing that finally got him into eternal trouble one stormy day long ago.

One morning, the upright Boston man went to visit friends in Concord, taking his young daughter along with him for a special treat. He solemnly promised his anxious wife that they would return before nightfall, since she did not like to be alone in the house after dark. After finishing their visit, Peter Rugg and his daughter embarked upon their return journey in an open chaise with plenty of time to spare, but a sudden storm swept over the town now known as West Cambridge, forcing them take shelter in a local tavern owned by a friend.

As daylight waned and the storm gave no sign of abating, Peter's famous temper got the better of him. When his friend urged them to stay the night rather than brave the storm, Peter cried, "I gave m'wife m'word, and I'll not break it!" When the friend pressed him on the matter, Peter let forth a string of curse words that made his friend's face turn bright red. Peter stomped about in a circle, and his wig turned sideways as he danced from foot to foot in growing rage. Finally, he caught his daughter by the hand and marched out the door into the downpour, shouting, "Let the storm increase! I'll see my home tonight despite this foul tempest, or may I never see home again!"

WHICH WAY TO BOSTON?

With these words, Peter Rugg tossed his shivering, soaking-wet daughter into her seat, righted his soggy wig, leapt in beside the little girl, and whipped up his horses. A moment later, he was gone, bound for Boston. He never arrived.

Mrs. Rugg waited in vain, that night and many more, for her Peter and her little girl to arrive. Searchers could trace him only as far as the friend's tavern and no further. Finally, the two were given up for dead and mourned accordingly.

But not long after the memorial services occurred, neighbors in that particular Boston block started hearing the sound of a chaise racing up the street on stormy nights. The noise of its passage rattled their doors, and some claimed to hear the crack of a whip and a voice that sounded like that of Peter Rugg, swearing fiercely as he searched in vain for the house from which his spirit was barred.

Soon, reports of a fast-driving carriage containing the furious, soaking-wet Rugg and his little daughter started pouring in from all over the state, and then from as far away as Connecticut and New York. Folks meeting the odd pair said that Rugg always stopped to ask directions to Boston but was never able to follow them correctly, often heading in exactly the opposite direction from the one pointed out to him. His little daughter never said a word during these encounters. And for hours after such a visitation, a fierce storm would rage over the vicinity.

One unfortunate toll collector manning the Charlestown Bridge frequently heard the chaise rushing past his toll-house at the height of each storm that broke over the area. One night he finally summoned up the courage to rush out into the thunder and lightning to confront the toll-breaker, standing at the center of the bridge and holding a three-legged stool before him like a sword. Horse, carriage, man, and girl came barreling toward him without stopping. At the very last moment, he leapt aside with a shout and flung the stool at the horse. He watched in amazement as the stool went right through the black creature and landed on the far side of the bridge. Then the careening carriage disappeared into the darkness on the other side.

Long after his wife and all his friends were dead and forgotten, the spirit of Peter Rugg and his daughter traveled on, searching for a way back to their Boston home. Reports of this strange, traveling pair have continued to this day, keeping the tale alive in the minds of all those living roundabout Northampton. Or so went the story that the modern-day "Peter Rugg" learned as a child.

Since that Peter also had a bad habit of swearing whenever he lost his temper, his wife Mandy had started fining him 25 cents every time he uttered one of the words on her "black list."

"I don't want our son learning any colorful language at such a young and impressionable age," she scolded her husband after their little boy had parroted a very colorful word one morning when Mandy put him down for a nap. Conceding her point, Peter had reluctantly adhered to the new ruling handed down by his suddenly fierce wife.

"Dang," he shouted now at his errant car, substituting a word that had not been blackballed by his wife. It didn't have the power and pizzazz of his favorite swear words, but at least it helped express his feelings a bit. "Dang! Dang! Dang!" Peter repeated. He slammed the car into park, touched the hood release button, and then nipped out into the drizzle to stare gloomily down at his engine. He'd always meant to take an auto-repair and maintenance class in school but had never gotten around to it. Too caught up in sports and academics. And a doctoral degree in history wasn't any help out here on a desolate side road with a broken-down car.

"Double dang and blast!" Peter said, dropping the hood down again and climbing back into the car. The softly falling rain had already saturated his clothing, and he shivered as he tried in vain to restart the car. The engine ground a few times but wouldn't turn over. Great. He pulled out his cell phone to call Mandy and realized with a groan that he was in a dead zone.

Peter said a word that was definitely on his wife's black list and shoved the phone back into his pocket. He used some more colorful language and had racked up a two-dollar fine by the time he heard the wild sound of a galloping horse and the rattling, clinking noise of a carriage coming down the road. He blinked at the unaccustomed sound. To his knowledge, none of his neighbors owned horses, nor did anyone else in this vicinity. And those folks who rode horses didn't drive carriages anymore. These days, carriage driving was a specialty sport.

Peter glanced out the back window, but it had fogged up when the car stalled. He rolled down the window next to the driver's seat and peered out into the growing darkness. He saw the light of a carriage lantern shaking and bobbing toward him at an alarming pace in the rain-swept dusk, creating strange patterns on the trees at the bend in the road. A moment later, a black horse raced around the curve, pulling an open carriage in which sat a soaking-wet man in an old-fashioned wig, cloak, and hat, clutching the horse's reigns in his large hands. Beside him sat a shivering little girl.

Within moments, the carriage had drawn close to the stalled car. Peter gasped as his eyes met those of a wet, weary, anxiety-driven man who looked so exhausted that Peter thought he might topple over. "Which way to Boston?" the man called from the carriage, slowing the black horse for a moment to speak to him.

Peter was struck by chills from head to toe as he simultaneously recognized both question and speaker. He opened his mouth and shut it again, like a startled codfish, but couldn't summon up any words.

The anxious man in the carriage let forth a blistering spate of curse words and then shouted: "Speak up, man! Which way to Boston? We must reach Boston by nightfall!"

Mutely, unable to speak for sheer fear and astonishment, Peter pointed back the way the carriage had come. But the man in the carriage did not heed him. He slapped the reigns against the horse's flank and urged it down the isolated road that led away from his stated destination. A moment later, carriage, horse, and ghosts had disappeared around the next bend in the road.

Peter leaned back against his seat, gasping in shock. Had he . . . had he just seen the ghost of Peter Rugg? Above him, the sky was suddenly split by a fierce bolt of lightning, and static electricity prickled his skin. The thunderclap shook his car, and he had barely enough time to raise his window before the rain came pouring down upon him.

Storm-bringer, Peter thought to himself, remembering his folklore. The first Peter Rugg was called the Storm-bringer, and right on schedule, here was the storm. He felt cold all over, and his body shook with the shock of his ghostly encounter.

At that moment, the sharp shrill of a car horn made him jump. Heart thudding so hard against his chest that it hurt, he glanced out his window and recognized the large SUV owned by Rick, his next-door neighbor. Peter rolled down his window and Rick shouted, "Car trouble?"

Peter replied in the affirmative and gratefully accepted a ride home. Grabbing his briefcase, he made a mad dash through the heavy rain, pausing only long enough to click the electronic control that locked his car before slamming breathlessly into the passenger seat of the SUV.

Rick put the car in gear and started slowly off through the heavy rain toward home. "What's wrong with your car?" he asked Peter.

"The repair light came on and the engine won't turn over," Peter replied.

"Good thing I came along, or you might have found yourself swearing to reach home before dawn and driving the roads of Massachusetts for eternity, just like the other Peter Rugg," Rick joked.

Peter gave a feeble chuckle, his arms prickling at the remembrance of the ghost he had seen.

"Mandy made me give up swearing," he said, changing the subject. "Wants to make sure I set a good example for the boy."

This confession made Rick laugh heartily, and the subject occupied them the rest of the way home.

The only person Peter told about his ghostly encounter was his wide-eyed wife, and her only response to the story was to hold him close and whisper, "See? Aren't you glad I made you give up swearing?"

And in that moment, Peter Rugg certainly was.

3

The Missing Bride

The village was astir long before the first rays of the midsummer sunrise beamed through the treetops and flickered across the rippling waters of the lake. Giggling girls and beaming women were cooking up a great feast, and the nervous young chief Sassacus was pacing back and forth inside his home while his mother followed him around and fussed over his wedding clothes.

In all the hustle and bustle, no one noticed the beautiful young bride, Iano, slipping out of the village and heading toward the glittering waters of the lake. She was both nervous and excited and wished to take a paddle in her canoe to calm her prewedding jitters. And no one noticed Wequoash, her rejected suitor, quietly following her in his own canoe.

It was only when a few of Iano's friends and family came to help her dress for her wedding that the bride was found to be missing. No one was unduly alarmed, for Iano loved to play hide-and-seek with her beloved chief, and everyone assumed she was waiting for him to hunt her down and swing her up in his arms as he always did when he found her.

Chuckling to himself, Sassacus checked all the usual hiding places, to no avail. As the day wore on, he became alarmed. A serious search was made, and a canoe was found missing. Into the hubbub came Wequoash, a mighty panther slung across his shoulders that he had hunted down and killed as a present for the chief and his bride. Casting the cat aside, he joined the hunt, expressing every bit as much alarm as the chief himself. But Iano was nowhere to be found.

For two long days the tribesmen searched and the women wept and kept watch. At the end of the second day, the body of Iano was taken from the lake by a weeping Sassacus. All the tribe gathered to mourn the passing of the fair maiden, and none wept louder or more convincingly than Wequoash. As for the chief, he stood ashen-faced and shaking at the graveside and collapsed a few days later, so stricken was his heart.

Wequoash, the mighty hunter, stayed steadfastly by the side of his ailing chief. When Sassacus succumbed to his illness at week's end, Wequoash stumbled forth from the sickbed, wailing mightily, and blamed himself for failing to save the life of his chief.

After observing the death rights for their fallen leader, the tribe elected Wequoash to be the new chief, and he modestly accepted the honor. The time of mourning soon ended, and life went on as usual in the village. The pain of Sassacus and Iano's sudden passing was put aside in the face of the daily activities of the tribe, and the pair were spoken of infrequently.

In midsummer of the following year, Wequoash was standing idly on the shore of the lake when he saw a mighty flame spring up at its very center. He stared at it in astonishment, and fear raised the hair on his arms and sent shivers crawling across the back of his neck. At that moment, a canoe materialized beside the flame and came racing across the waters toward the stunned warrior. Before he could blink, it was bobbing in the shallow waters next to him.

A cold breeze swept around Wequoash and seized his arms and legs, propelling him forward toward the canoe. As his feet splashed into the shallow waters, he fought the compulsion, struggling against the wind that forced him forward. But it was too strong, and it toppled him into the canoe in an instant. By the time he righted himself, he was skimming across the lake toward the flickering fire. The canoe stopped right in front of the flames, which grew stronger and taller until they towered above him, taking on the glowing aspect of Iano. Wequoash shrieked in terror and cowered in the bottom of the canoe. The flaming figure of the missing bride reached down toward him, and he blacked out. When he awoke, he found himself lying half-in and half-out of the water on the shore.

Wequoash leapt to his feet with a yelp and ran toward the village. At the outskirts he paused, took a deep breath, and sauntered toward his wigwam as if nothing had happened. It was only when he stepped inside that he realized that it was exactly one year ago that Iano had drowned. He shuddered once from head to toe, and then pushed the incident out of his mind.

Another year passed, and the village prospered under the leadership of Wequoash. Many of the eligible girls vied for his attention, but he chose none to be his bride. As midsummer approached again, Wequoash grew moody and silent. Something seemed to be weighing on his mind, but no one could discover what it was.

On the anniversary of Iano's death, Wequoash went hunting in the opposite direction of the lake, wanting no more visions or strange occurrences to haunt him. Yet this mighty hunter

THE MISSING BRIDE

suddenly found himself lost in the woods he had known all of his life. He circled around and around, unable to find his way. When he burst forth at last from the underbrush, he was on the shores of the lake near his village. And in the center of the lake he saw the mighty, flaming figure of Iano.

Wequoash was not surprised when a black canoe appeared out of nowhere and whooshed across the lake to bob before him. He was not surprised when a cold wind whipped around him and thrust him unceremoniously into the boat. He had lived through all of this before. When he reached the center of the lake, the massive, flaming figure of Iano bent over him and said: "Only one time more."

Wequoash stared up at the flaming figure, mesmerized, his head swimming. He was not aware of losing consciousness, but he must have, for his next waking memory was of lying on the shore with his feet in the water and his head pillowed on a rock. He sat up slowly, trembling in fear. With a heavy heart he made his way home.

The next year did not go well for the village. Wequoash was too preoccupied to participate in the councils, and he rarely hunted or fished. He grew thin and weak and withdrew into himself, snapping at friends and family alike. No one could discover what ailed him. As midsummer drew closer, Wequoash retreated completely and refused to come out of his wigwam. Everyone in the village was alarmed and fearful, and no one knew what to do.

Then, on midsummer day, Wequoash appeared suddenly in the doorway and called out loudly for his people to gather. Wondering, uneasy, the villagers came to him, and the chief held his hands up for silence.

"Today is my death day," he announced, and waited to continue until the startled murmurs died away. "Three years ago, I followed Iano when she paddled her canoe across the lake in the early morning of her wedding day. I was jealous and bitter at losing her to another, and so I tipped her canoe over and left her to drown. Then when Sassacus, your chief, fell ill, I poisoned him and let him die."

There were gasps of outrage from his people, but he waved them silent. "The time has come. Today I will pay for my deeds. See there," he added, pointing toward the lake. "The spirit of Iano comes for me!"

Everyone turned and saw a mighty pillar of flame burst forth from the waters of the lake. Wequoash stepped among his people and they shied away from him superstitiously as he marched toward the shore of the lake. The black canoe zipped across the water and bobbed in the shallows. Without a murmur, Wequoash allowed the breeze to sweep him inside, and his people watched as the canoe rushed forward, carrying their chief toward the flaming figure of Iano.

As Wequoash reached the place where Iano had drowned, a massive bolt of lightning crashed down from the heavens and enveloped the canoe in light. The clap of thunder that followed it flattened all those who had followed their chief to the shore. When they stumbled, trembling, to their feet, the canoe containing Wequoash was gone.

From that day onward, the villagers carried small stones with them when they crossed the lake and were careful to drop them at the place where Wequoash died as a memorial to appease the spirits of the dead who haunted that location. The memorial pillar can be seen on the bottom of the lake to this day.

4

The Treasure and the Cats

IPSWICH

Old Harry Main, the sandman, was grumbling and moaning at the sandbar as the boy slipped out of his home, shovel in one hand and lantern in the other. In life, Harry Main had been a pirate and a wrecker who had caused the death of many sailors, luring their ships with false lights so that they ran aground on the Ipswich bar, where he now forever did penance for his crimes. According to local folklore, Main twined ropes of sand in his transparent hands and used them to push back the sea. When tide and gale beset the land, as it had last night, Harry Main would howl and moan on the bar as the wild waves washed away his sand-structures and broke his rope.

The moon was small and high that night, and the boy barely needed the lantern as he walked silently down the path toward the beach. Harry Main was large in his thoughts, not because he pitied the eternal sandman, but because he coveted the treasure Main had buried somewhere along those shores. During the storm, while the wind howled and the rain lashed and old Harry moaned on the bar as towering waves pummeled and slapped it, the boy had lain dreaming in his bed. In his dream, he saw Harry Main's evil, glowing ghost slipping from his shackles on the sandbar to check on his treasure. The boy had followed the specter and had seen for himself the location of the buried chests full of gold. And when he woke, he remembered. And wondered.

The gale raged for three days and three nights. And each night of the storm, the boy had dreamed the same dream of old Harry Main and the treasure. After the third night, the boy was determined to dig up the ill-gotten gains of the pirate and claim them as his own.

Tonight, he had gathered his courage and slipped away once his boisterous, happy family were all in bed asleep. The boy's destination was an abandoned mill not far from the shore. It lay rotting and ruined in a copse of trees, vines twining everywhere and trees growing through gaps in its walls. The wind wailed through the tops of the pines and whistled eerily among the dead timbers of the decrepit old mill.

The boy shivered superstitiously when he caught sight of the looming building, which glared at him through black gaps in the wood that looked like the empty eyes of a skull. He stood trembling at the edge of the trees, wishing he had thought to bring his Bible as protection against this foul spot. In his mind, he saw again the ghastly, pale-blue ghost flickering madly as it walked through the gale to this place to check on its treasure. Old Harry Main. The boy's knees buckled and he nearly fled at the memory; his heart beating so fast that it hurt his chest.

With trembling fingers, he adjusted the wick of the lantern to give him more light, drew in a deep breath, and started shakily for the mill. Only the picture in his mind of the ghost of Harry Main staring in satisfaction down at two huge treasure chests kept him moving forward. When something brushed his leg in the sagging doorway of the mill, the boy screamed aloud, bumping into the frame and driving a sharp splinter into his arm. He looked frantically around for the source of the contact, his whole body rigid with terror, pulse pounding madly and skin clammy. Then his darting eyes rested on a small, furry black cat that mewed up at him daintily, and he relaxed and laughed shakily.

"You scared me, puss," the boy said, stooping down to pat her on the head. The cat purred and nudged her head against his hand.

Feeling relieved, the boy made his way across the rotting floor to the place where he'd seen the ghost of Harry Main gazing down upon his treasure. Setting the lantern carefully on a ledge, he started digging. He was a large boy who did most of the heavy chores around the house and barn, so he did not flinch from his task, knowing that a few hours of digging would bring him treasure beyond his wildest dreams.

Digging the pit was a hard, sweaty job that required his total concentration and allowed no room for dire imaginings or fear. Soon ghost, black cat, and the eerie whooshing of the wind in the rafters were forgotten as he dug deeper and deeper. And then his shovel struck something solid.

Breathless with excitement, the boy worked faster and soon cleared the debris away from a large, flat stone with a handle carved into it. His heart beat very fast against his ribs as he stared down at the stone handle. He became aware that the sound of the wind in the rafters had changed. It had grown higher in pitch and taken on the keen of many voices chanting in a language he did not know. The sound made the hairs on his arms and neck stand on end, and his skin prickled. Then the flickering glow of lantern-light on stone was replaced by a strange red light beaming down on him from above, and he felt a pair of eyes staring at him.

Suddenly, he remembered that he had company in this foul, abandoned place. A cat had entered the building with him. A *black* cat.

The boy swallowed hard in dismay and then looked up toward the rim of the pit in which he stood. And saw the cat, now large as a lion, its red eyes glowing with the fires of hell. Beside it stood another beast, and yet another. Black cats surrounded the pit, glaring down at him with foul red eyes, each one larger than its brother, no matter which way you counted. One caught the boy's eye and yawned, displaying fangs the size of his forearm. The boy fell to his knees, his trembling legs unable to support him.

As he gazed mesmerized at the cats, the light from behind him began shifting again, first glowing red and then turning into the flickering blue that he remembered from his dreams. Some deep animal instinct told him that the ghost of Harry Main was right behind him. And he knew the specter was angry. Sheer horror stiffened the boy's backbone and gave strength to his shaking legs. He leapt to his feet, waved his arms at the ferocious felines lining the rim of the pit and shouted: "Scat! Scat, I say."

Then he whirled to face the phantom, which loomed higher and higher above him, its ghastly bearded face and half-blind eyes reaching up to the sagging roof.

"Who disturbs my treasure?" Old Harry Main boomed, and a bolt of lightning slammed out of the clear sky into the decaying roof of the mill. Thunder clapped right over the boy's

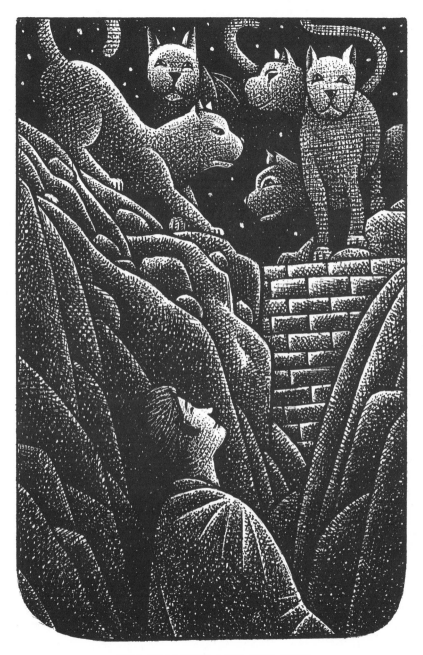

THE TREASURE AND THE CATS

head, and sour, icy-cold salt water began pouring into the pit the boy had dug, rapidly filling it. The boy gasped and scrabbled against the torrent which tried to pull him down and drown him. A desperate leap brought his hand in contact with a strong root. This gave him enough purchase against the muddy flood to pull himself out of the pit.

The boy ran out of the mill and out of the woods, covered from head to toe in mud, his lantern and shovel forgotten. Behind him, a second bolt of lightning hit the abandoned mill. And as he reached the safety of the seashore and raced for home, the old mill began to burn.

It was a seven-day wonder in town how the old mill had come to burn to the ground on a clear night after having its old boards soaked for three days by a terrible storm. Whenever anyone spoke of it, the boy turned pale and started trembling. His parents wondered at this sudden attack of nerves in their normally cocky son but put it down to his having a slight touch of cold. As for the boy, he never again went near the copse of trees with the burned husk of the mill at its center. And for the rest of his life, he would walk a mile out of his way rather than cross paths with a black cat.

5

A Basket of Cod

PLYMOUTH

"Polly! Ahoy, Polly!"

The sound of my name ringing through the busy marketplace brought me to a halt. I whirled, heart racing with excitement as I recognized the beloved voice. It was Joe, my Joe, calling my name. Which was a bit puzzling, since he was supposed to be out on the banks with his captain-father on a month-long fishing trip. Yet here he came, tripping through the crowd toward me with a basket of cod on his arm.

I was thrilled to see him. A storm had come up a few nights before that had whipped the ocean into a sea of high waves, and I had sat up most of the night picturing Joe and his father fighting the waves in the *Miranda Lee*. She was a stout ship, but that storm was a killer.

I ran forward and hugged Joe tight, smelly basket of fish notwithstanding. I was used to it by now. Some swains wooed their ladies with pretty words and flowers. My Joe didn't talk much and came a-wooing with baskets of fish and crabs and other creatures of the sea. Not as pretty as flowers, but my parents and I had sat down to many a good meal since my Joe took a fancy to me.

As I pulled back a little, I studied him. Blond hair cut unfashionably short, and twinkling blue eyes that seemed to see right into my soul. They laughed at me now as he stole a kiss right in the middle of the street.

"Rascal," I laughed, fending him off as pretty pink color flooded my cheeks. "What would Mother say?"

Unrepentant, he ran a work-roughened hand through my black curls and caressed my cheek. "What would Mother say?" he repeated mockingly, swinging the basket of fish to his other hip so he could pull me close.

"It's a good thing we are already betrothed," I said severely, submitting to a second kiss. "Or Father would haul us before the preacher this instant!"

Joe laughed and hugged me so tight I could barely breathe. And for a flash of a moment, I sensed a deep pain inside him, an unbearable longing that I did not understand. It shook me to the core, and I held him tighter, trying to push myself inside him and take the pain away.

"Oh, Polly, my Polly," Joe whispered against my hair. "Remember how much I love you."

Then he broke away, thrust the basket of fish into my arms, and vanished without a trace. I was astonished. One moment he was right in front of me, and the next gone, as if he had never been there. If it weren't for the smelly basket of fish in my arms, he might have been a dream.

Forgetting all about the errands that brought me to town, I headed back home with the fish, wishing that my arms would stop pricking. Shivers were running up and down my spine in dread of the wordless something I had sensed when Joe hugged me that last time. And why had he said those words: "Remember how much I love you"? Of course I would remember. We were getting married next month.

My parents were surprised and pleased by the gift of cod that Joe had sent, but puzzled that he hadn't accompanied me home and stayed to dinner. Father decided that Joe must have been needed on the docks to help unload the ship. This sounded sensible to me, until I remembered the strange way that he had vanished right before my eyes.

The next morning brought a knock on the door from a neighbor. His face was sober, and he barely looked at Mother and me, but hurried Father into the study and shut the door. For a few minutes, there was just the muffled sound of low voices. Then Father emerged with our neighbor behind him. He came over to me and took my hands soberly, and I read the message in his face even before he spoke.

"Joe is gone, Polly," he said sadly, his eyes bright with unshed tears. "The *Miranda Lee* went down in the storm a few nights ago. She was capsized by a massive wave that wrecked nearly half the boats fishing the banks that night."

Our neighbor nodded sadly. His ship was one of the few that had successfully ridden out the storm. He had seen the *Miranda Lee* go down with his own eyes but had been too far away to help—had help even been possible in such a storm.

The whole room started spinning, and the world turned gray before my eyes. Father and Mother helped me to a chair. By the time things came back into focus, our neighbor had tactfully taken himself away.

My poor mind spun, trying to understand that Joe was gone, but it couldn't. Then my eyes widened and I stared up at

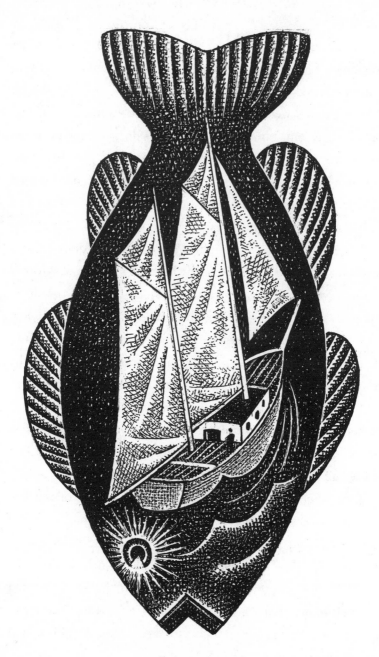

A BASKET OF COD

Father: "Joe can't be dead!" I cried. "I saw him yesterday. He gave me that basket of cod!"

Mother gasped then and began to sob. And Father, glancing sadly at her, brushed his hand against my cheek—just as Joe had done yesterday—and said: "Polly, the basket of cod vanished as soon as your Mother set it down on the kitchen table. The fish we ate last night came from the marketplace. We were afraid to tell you, afraid of what it might mean."

It was then that I finally grasped what my parents were saying. It had been Joe's ghost who had visited me in the market yesterday, come to say farewell. Remembering how he had held me close, and the sensation of longing that I had sensed in him, I knew that he—wherever he was—was as saddened by our parting as I.

"Remember how much I love you," Joe had said.

And I always would.

6

Hoosac Tunnel

NORTH ADAMS

I was working for the railroad company back in those days. They'd taken on a huge project, building a five-mile tunnel through the Berkshires that would directly connect Boston with Troy, New York, and they needed plenty of workers to assist them—especially after the fancy boring machine they first brought in got stuck in the hard rock and couldn't do the job.

Emma and I had just been married and were hoping to have us a couple of kids sometime in the near future. In the meantime, we settled into a nice house in a town close to the tunnel, and Emma set up housekeeping and started helping out in the sewing circle and the Ladies Aid Society at church. She was happy as a clam, and I was happy to come home to her embrace each night after the dirty, rough work in the tunnel.

Frankly, my work in the "great bore" worried my little bride. We were blasting with nitro, and a lot of fellows had gotten killed. A couple of years back two chaps died in a blast when the explosive was touched off prematurely. The man responsible for their deaths—Ringo Kelley—up and disappeared afterward. No one knew what became of the man until he showed up dead in the tunnel a year to the day after the event. He'd been strangled.

I started work shortly after Kelley's corpse was found, and my coworkers took delight in telling me the gruesome tale and promising me that it was the ghosts of the two dead miners who had strangled Kelley. But I was skeptical. Of course, I could understand why such tales had gotten about. The tunnel seemed cursed by bad luck. After the boring machine was abandoned, the company was forced to begin the project again in a different spot, this time using manpower and nitro. It was a huge undertaking. The "bloody pit"—a nickname given to the Hoosac Tunnel—was going to be nearly five miles long and would bore underneath mountains that were nearly two thousand feet high. Teams of men were digging into the mountains from both ends, and somehow they would have to meet in the middle.

I was working on the east portal of the tunnel. Every day, I'd walk into the damp, chilly expanse, the lantern I carried making a shadowy, flickering kind of light that was hard on the eyes. The tunnel echoed strangely, carrying some words for miles and suppressing others. It was an eerie place, and I didn't wonder that the men believed it haunted. I sometimes felt that way myself when a chill breeze swept down on me out of the darkness overhead, raising goose bumps on my arms and legs.

After a few months, I was reassigned to work on a central shaft that the engineers had dreamed up. We would bore downward toward the center of the tunnel from a point on the western ridge, just a few hundred feet above the lowest section of the valley between the mountains. From there, teams could begin blasting east and west and meet up with the teams working

HOOSAC TUNNEL

at either end. The central shaft—planned as a thousand-foot vertical air conduit—would also be kitted out as a workers' entrance. When it was done, a large bucket would be attached at the top that would be used to lower workers down to the center of the tunnel. But the construction of the shaft went awry suddenly on October 19, 1867.

I was working outside the shaft, carting away debris, when I heard an explosion. I rushed toward the shaft with a number of my fellow laborers, but we could see nothing but fire. Suddenly, four desperate men came scrambling upward toward us through the smoke and flames. We pulled them out of the blazing shaft and hurried them to safety before demanding explanations. Apparently, naphtha fumes from one of the lamps had triggered the explosion.

"The hoist house caught fire," wheezed one of the stricken men, shaking and coughing under the blanket I'd wrapped him in. "It collapsed into the shaft. Jim, there are thirteen men down there—nearly five hundred feet down! They must have been pummeled by the winching machinery. And dear God, there were three hundred newly sharpened drill bits in the house too!" He looked sickened at the thought of those sharpened bits raining down on the helpless men. He coughed again, trying to rid his lungs of smoke, and accepted a drink of water.

He was too stunned at that moment to realize the other implications of the accident. The explosion would have taken out both the water and air pumps that kept the shaft safe for the miners. With the fire rapidly consuming the air in the shaft, there soon would be no oxygen left, and those miners who did not suffocate would drown as the pit flooded with water. My stomach clenched and churned at the thought. But we couldn't get near the shaft while the fire raged. As soon as it was put out, a worker named Mallory was lowered into the shaft by rope to check on the men, but he had to be hauled up quickly because he was overcome by fumes. Eventually, we knew that the miners' time had just run out.

Emma was terrified when she learned of the disaster and the deaths of the workmen. Though she said nothing about it, I knew she didn't want me working the tunnel anymore. But we needed the money, and the doctor had confirmed we had a baby on the way, so I went back each day in spite of the danger.

I came to hate working near the drowned shaft. Sometimes I could hear muffled cries coming from the pit, even though everyone inside was long dead. And once in a while, I would see misty figures hovering over the watery hole in the ground. Seeing them made my flesh creep, but hearing the ghostly cries for help was much worse. There was nothing I could do to help the poor devils, and each time I heard the voices I wanted to run away and weep. Me—a big tough man, wanting to bawl like a baby.

It didn't take long for snow and fog to descend upon us. This made the situation much worse. One evening as I was finishing for the day, I looked up to see a line of miners walking toward the watery pit with axes and shovels slung across their broad shoulders. They were glowing with a soft white-blue light, and their feet were a good six inches above the snow. I stared at them, jaw agape, as they vanished without a trace, leaving only swirling mist and undisturbed snow. I backed away and ran from the pit as fast as my feet would carry me.

The next day, I requested a transfer to a different part of the tunnel. I wanted away from that haunted pit. The foreman took one look at my pale face and shaking hands and asked no questions. He moved me to a different location, and I spent the rest of the winter underground.

The pit wasn't fully drained of water until a year later. Thirteen bodies were recovered, and it was discovered that only a few had been killed by the falling drill bits and flaming debris. The survivors had actually erected a raft and floated partway up the shaft—but had died of asphyxiation from the same noxious gases that had nearly killed Mallory when we sent him down the shaft to search for them.

Em and I attended the funerals with our baby son. Afterward, one of my buddies who worked near the shaft reported that the ghostly visitations had ceased with the dead men's burial. I was glad to hear it but still refused to go near the place.

A month after the funerals, one of the men in town offered me a job working the counter at the mercantile for a higher wage than I was earning at the tunnel. I jumped at the chance, much to Emma's quiet relief, and that was the end of my career with the railroad. Sometime later, I heard the total death count during the construction of the Hoosac Tunnel was 193 workers.

Folks claim that the tunnel is still haunted by the ghost of Kelley and the other workers who lost their lives in its construction. Stories about headless haunts, ghostly lights, and weird voices are whispered to this day. Remembering the ghostly miners I'd seen near the drowned shaft, I cannot discount them. And I must admit that I've never taken a train ride through that tunnel. I've had enough of its horrors to last me a lifetime.

7

The Shroud

CAPE COD

My friend Ginny and I were thrilled when we found summer jobs out on Cape Cod. After a tough year at university, a summer vacation spent on the beach suited me just fine, and Ginny felt the same. I was a little worried, though, about where we were going to stay. Lodgings at the Cape weren't exactly cheap, and I didn't want all of my salary to go right back into accommodations. I would need money for textbooks and other college expenses next semester.

I'd just about given up hope on the Cape Cod caper and resigned myself to a job inland when a family friend gave me a call. She and her husband had just purchased an old house on the Cape but wouldn't be able to occupy it for a few months while her husband finished out his notice on his position in the Midwest. She'd heard that I was looking for a place and invited us to stay at her new home for the summer. What a relief! I jumped at the offer, and within a few weeks, Ginny and I were hauling our baggage through the front door of the residence—an old sea captain's house.

It was a lovely place with a large, comfortable living space downstairs and a nice kitchen. Ginny and I would be staying in the two upstairs bedrooms, and I chose the one at the head of the staircase. Ginny tripped down the hall to the second bedroom, which she declared to be just the ticket. It didn't take us long to settle in, and then we were off to the beach to do some sun-worshipping (and boy-watching). Dinner was just a few sandwiches and chips that first evening, since we didn't take time to shop before hitting the beach.

As we mounted the creaky staircase after our late supper, I felt a chill pass over my skin. I shivered a bit.

"Did you feel that draft?" I asked Ginny.

She glanced back at me from the top of the steps. "What draft?" she asked.

But the chill was gone, as suddenly as it had come. I shook my head at her. "Just the quirks of an old house," I replied.

I slept well that night, worn out from the move and the fresh air of the beach. The next day, Ginny and I started work serving tables at a local restaurant. We spent the day on our feet rushing around, and we didn't feel much like visiting the beach that first night after work. But we adjusted to the job and soon regained our energy and enthusiasm for the beach and other after-work pursuits.

About a week after we moved in, I was awakened from my sleep by the same chilly draft that I'd felt the first night on the staircase. My eyes flew open, and my heart started beating faster. Some ancient animal instinct told me to stay very, very still.

My bed was opposite the open bedroom door, and I could see straight across the hall and down the staircase. And what I saw froze every muscle in my body. Floating up the staircase was a tall, gray figure in a shroud. It glowed faintly. The folds and drapes of the shroud were whipping around as if blown by a silent gale. Dark shadows scuttled away under the flapping ends of the phantom's robes as it drifted quietly up one stair, and then two. It stayed near the wall, rising up the staircase as if it mounted them on heavy, invisible feet.

Around my bed, the air grew cold and colder. My whole body started shuddering under the light summer sheets, and I wanted to hide my head under the pillow. But that would be even worse, because then I wouldn't be able to see where the shrouded phantom went.

As I watched, panting softly in panic, the glowing ghost reached the top of the staircase. Turning, it drifted past my door and down the hall. My whole body tensed. Ginny's room was down the hall! What if that thing was after Ginny? I wanted to get up and race after it, to warn my friend of the danger. But I couldn't seem to move.

I'd read in books about people who couldn't move after receiving a fright, but I'd always discounted that as literary license taken by the author. Now I knew that it was true. My chest felt so tight that it hurt, my heart was throbbing against my ribs, and my stomach roiled in terror. The bed was shaking with my nervous trembling, and I knew my legs would not bear my weight if I tried to stand. I don't know how long I lay in terrified silence as the chilly wind slowly faded from the room. I must have fallen asleep eventually from sheer exhaustion, because the next thing I knew it was morning, and beautiful, blessed sunlight was dancing through the windows, wiping out the horror with its warmth.

Suddenly I remembered Ginny. I leapt from my bed and ran down the hall. Her room was empty, her bed obviously slept in. Then I heard her rattling around down in the kitchen, humming

THE SHROUD

a happy tune. I sighed with relief, went to fetch a bathrobe, and tumbled down the stairs to tell Ginny my story. My friend was polite but disbelieving.

"It was just a nightmare," she said, handing me a carton of milk. "Just a dream."

I shook my head. "I don't have nightmares," I stated flatly. "Never have, not even as a little kid."

"Well, you've had one now," Ginny said, plopping the cereal box on the table with a bang. "I didn't see or hear anything out of the ordinary last night."

"I'm telling you, I saw a ghost," I repeated.

"And I'm telling you, there's no such thing," Ginny said, sitting down at the table with her own cereal bowl. "Look, if it will make you feel better, I'll trade rooms with you."

I nodded vigorously, mouth full of cereal. Yes, that would make me feel much better. I still didn't like staying in a haunted house, but at least I'd be in a room that didn't have a ghost stalking past it in the middle of the night.

We traded bedrooms right after breakfast. As I settled into the back room, I felt as if a heavy weight had been removed from my chest. I gave a sigh of relief and changed into my uniform in preparation for work.

Two mornings later, Ginny came down to breakfast trembling, with dark circles under her eyes. I didn't need to ask what was wrong. I knew at once that she'd seen the shrouded figure mounting the staircase, just as I had. A simple query confirmed it.

"It was tall and faceless and gray," Ginny gasped, waving her hands to emphasize how tall, how faceless, how gray. "The robes flapped in a cold breeze that froze me right to the bone, and it glowed! But it was a dark glow, if you can understand that! And the shadows around it . . . ” Her voice trailed off and she collapsed into a chair.

“I am not staying in that room another night,” she told me. “Your turn.”

Now I was the one who turned pale and started shaking. “Not me!” I said.

“It’s either that or move out of this house,” Ginny said firmly. “And you know we can’t afford to do that.”

I had to concede her point. We were earning good salaries, but the money wouldn’t go far if we had to rent an apartment for the rest of the summer. If we could even find an apartment at this late date. So we traded rooms again.

I didn’t see the ghost for the first two nights, though you can bet that I didn’t sleep very well in that haunted room. On the third night, when the chilly breeze swept through the doorway, I knew what to expect. I’d debated sleeping with the door shut, but had decided that this would make things even worse. If I slept with the door shut, I wouldn’t be able to see the shrouded phantom coming until it was right in my room.

So I watched the glowing gray figure in the shapeless shroud as it rose up the staircase near the wall. Its robes were whipping fiercely in the cold breeze. This second viewing was no easier than the first. My body froze instantly, and the bed shook and rattled under my tense body as the ghost reached the top of the steps. For a moment its glowing form loomed in front of my door and filled my whole world to the exclusion of all else. Then it moved out of sight down the hall, and in a moment, the chilly breeze that heralded its presence was gone.

That was it for me. I didn't sleep a wink the rest of the night. As soon as my trembling legs had steadied enough to hold me, I got up and started packing my bags. When a rumpled, sleepy-eyed Ginny appeared in my doorway the next morning, I told her that we were leaving. I didn't care how expensive it was, I wasn't staying here another night. Ginny didn't even argue.

In the end, we gave up our jobs on the Cape and went home. It was easier and cheaper, and it didn't take either of us long to find summer vacancies and earn the money we both needed for the next semester.

A few months after my generous friend and her husband moved into the house on the Cape, I got a call at school. After a few preliminary remarks, my friend hesitantly asked me if Ginny or I had seen anything strange while we were in the house. I knew at once what she meant, and told her about the shrouded figure that climbed the staircase during the night. She gave a gasp of relief when she heard that she and her husband weren't the only ones to have had a ghostly encounter. Then she told me that her teenage brother had been awakened one night by the chilly presence of something in his room, and that several other strange occurrences made her suspect that they were sharing their new home with a ghost.

A dig into the town files uncovered the story of a captain lost at sea and of a waiting wife who never accepted his loss. Some said that the wife still haunted the house and grounds, forever waiting for her lost husband to come home. Others said that it was the sea captain himself. I didn't know which story to believe. Something was haunting the house on the Cape, but I had no intention of going back there to find out which specter it was.

My friend and her husband were evidently not comfortable sharing their home with a ghost, because they sold it quickly and moved into an unhaunted house. I sometimes wonder what the new owners make of the shroud on the staircase, but I've never gone back to ask.

8

Lost My Head

AMESBURY

I was nearly knocked off my crutches in the flurry of excitement that heralded my arrival in Amesbury. I'd been fighting overseas for several years—most recently in France—and had been injured in the terrible D-Day invasion. I lost a leg below the knee and was lucky I hadn't lost my life, as had so many of the other boys in my unit. As soon as I was well enough, they sent me home. There was talk of giving me a false leg, but in the meantime I was getting by with a crutch. Best of all, it turned out that my sweetheart didn't care about my lost leg as long as the rest of me was back safe in her arms.

For the first several days home, I stayed with my parents in their new house in Amesbury. They'd moved to town a year after I was sent overseas, buying a house right next door to my sweetheart, which suited me just fine. Sally came over every night when she finished work to cuddle with me on the couch and plan our wedding.

My cousins and my aunt and uncle stayed away after that first night to give me time alone with my folks, but I knew they were itching to see me. About a week after my return, Sally drove me to their house on the other side of town for a visit.

Giving me a fond kiss, Sally headed out for the shops to get more of the fripperies she deemed necessary for our wedding, leaving me to visit with the folks. And visit we did. My aunt talked nonstop for two blessed hours in her attempt to fill me in on all the local goings-on that I'd missed. Uncle nodded and put in a word now and then when she stopped to draw breath, and the little cousins bounced off and on my lap and played with my crutch, pretending it was a machine gun. We had a lovely time.

Sally phoned at dusk to say she'd been delayed at the dress shop where she was being fitted for her wedding gown. I told her not to bother coming by. The dress shop wasn't too far away, and I wanted to get some exercise, so I told her I'd walk downtown and meet her there. Sally sounded a bit worried by this decision but didn't argue. She knew how much I hated losing the leg and respected my need for independence. Auntie, dear soul, didn't quite get it, but Uncle put a stop to her protests and waved me off from the front porch.

Auntie rushed up beside Uncle at the last moment and shouted, "Be careful of the ghost. He walks the streets around this time, looking for his head."

I laughed aloud and waved my crutch at her. A ghost! What nonsense. After the horrors I'd seen on the battlefield, a ghost didn't faze me one bit.

The air was crisp and a little cool for June, and the birds were chirping sleepily in the trees as I strolled down the road. Lights were going on in the houses, and I could hear the voices of mothers calling their children to supper and dogs barking a happy welcome as husbands and fathers came home from work.

My good leg wasn't used to so much exercise and was beginning to ache, so I slowed my pace. The streetlamps were making a pleasant glow along the brick sidewalk as I drew closer to the center of town. The road was oddly bereft of traffic that evening, and for some reason I felt a little strange walking down the lonesome street. I found my skin prickling, and I picked up the pace, in spite of my aching thigh and the sore place in my armpit where the crutch was rubbing me the wrong way. I scolded myself for being a ninny. Obviously, Auntie's talk about ghosts had spooked me more than I realized.

It was with some relief that I saw a tall figure round a corner and head down the street toward me. I was glad I was no longer alone. Or was I? For some reason, I couldn't get a good look at the fellow who was approaching so quickly. The streetlamps did nothing to illuminate his features. He seemed always to be moving in the dark shadows between each one. My heart started beating faster, and I had a sudden longing for the gun that had been my constant companion overseas.

This is nonsense, I thought to myself, getting a firm grip on my crutch and quickening my pace. After facing down the enemy on the beaches of Normandy, walking past a fellow citizen of my hometown should be nothing. As I scolded myself, I stepped right into a cold spot and stopped dead in my tracks, flesh creeping with the knowledge that something was very, very wrong. That was the moment that the man came abreast of me on the road. My heart gave a tremendous thud and started racing as my mind tried to take in what my eyes were seeing. The man was dressed in the rough uniform of a Revolutionary War soldier, and he was carrying his bloody head under one arm.

My jaw dropped open in shock and I let out a scream. Losing my head as completely as my fellow soldier, I fled down

LOST MY HEAD

the road, using a sort of running-hop to get me out of that cold spot. I had no idea I could make such good time on a crutch. In less than two seconds I had hopped past the headless soldier, skidded around the bend in the road, and was trotting rapidly through the hustle and bustle of downtown.

Sally was standing on the bench in the center of the dressmaker's shop, gowned in white from head to toe, when I dashed in the door. I slammed it shut behind me and leaned against it, panting with fear and exhaustion.

"Nick, you're not supposed to see the dress before the wedding," the dressmaker—an old family friend—scolded through the pins clenched in her lips. But Sally wasn't concerned about a silly old tradition. She could see that I was in a panic.

"Nick, what's wrong?" she demanded, gathering up her white skirts and stepping carefully down from the bench. "You look like you've seen a ghost!"

Hearing the "g" word made me panic all over again. With a wordless shout of terror, I bolted back out the door and into the street. I think I would have run-hopped all the way home if I hadn't spotted Sally's car parked on the next corner. I dodged through two trucks, rushed across the road, and flung myself into the passenger's seat. I hate to confess this, but I actually grabbed the blanket we kept in the back and flung it over my head, crouching down until I was curled up in a ball with most of my body on the floor under the dashboard.

A moment later the passenger door was wrenched open, and Sally peered down at me. By this time, the warmth of the blanket and the familiarity of Sally's car had begun calming my frazzled nerves. Feeling a bit sheepish, I slowly pulled my head out from under the blanket and looked up at her.

"Nick, what's wrong?" Sally repeated, half in fear and half in frustration.

"Nothing dear," I said as calmly as I could. "I just lost my head for a minute."

Then I started laughing hysterically and only stopped when Sally kissed me on the mouth.

"You wait right here and don't move," she commanded. "I've just got to change out of this dress, and then I'm taking you home."

I nodded silently and resumed huddling under the dashboard while my beautiful sweetheart raced back across the busy street in her wedding dress to explain to the dressmaker that she was marrying a crazy man. She was back within ten minutes, and she hauled me up from under the dashboard and made me sit properly in the seat before turning on the engine and heading for home.

Hesitantly at first, afraid that she was going to call off the wedding when she found out how crazy I was, I told her about seeing the headless soldier walking the streets of Amesbury at dusk. To my surprise, she nodded several times during the story, and when I was done she said: "I've seen him a couple of times myself. My Dad thinks he was beheaded by a cannonball sometime during the Revolutionary War. People have been seeing the ghost hereabouts for more than a hundred years. He never harms anyone, though; he just walks the streets at night, carrying his head."

I shuddered at the memory. "I tell you what, sweetie. I've seen some terrible things in my time, but the sight of that ghost ranks right up there as one of the scariest!"

"Worse than Normandy?" Sally asked me with a sideways glance as she pulled in our driveway.

Remembering that terrible day, I slowly shook my head. "That was a different kind of fear," I said grimly, and Sally—bless her heart—didn't ask me to explain. She just held the door for me as I pulled my sore body out of the car and promised to massage the pain out of my shoulders when we got inside. I caught her close and gave her a proper kiss, right there in front of the house.

"Thanks for believing me," I whispered in her ear.

"Thanks for coming home safe," she whispered back.

9

The Hitchhiker

REHOBOTH

My wife and I were always kidding our best friends about the hitchhiker. Josh and Sandy were firm believers in ghosts and claimed to have seen the mysterious red-haired phantom that was said to haunt Route 44. We sat at diner late one Saturday night, discussing the matter seriously. At least, Josh and Sandy were being serious. For Jill and I, it was a different matter.

"Funny how we've never seen him, and we drive that stretch of road all the time," my wife Jill drawled, blinking her long, dark eyelashes in an inane manner that made me grin.

"Probably because we're not crazy enough to believe in ghosts," I said, egging her on.

"Are you calling me crazy?" Josh asked, with a mock frown.

"Hey, bro', I wouldn't say anything to your face that I wouldn't say behind your back," I retorted.

"You skeptic," Sandy called from her seat across the table, emphasizing the word as if it were a curse. "I'll learn ya!" She waved her fist dramatically in the air, making Jill and I laugh even harder. "One of these days, Jerry, you're gonna find out I'm right. And you'll owe me a pizza. One of the large ones with everything on it!"

"If I ever see the ghostly hitchhiker, I'll buy you a large pizza every day for a year," I promised. "With everything on it!"

We bantered a bit more about the ghost, but I could tell Sandy and Josh were getting annoyed, so I turned the conversation to a less controversial topic while we ordered dessert. The evening ended pleasantly, and it wasn't long before Jill and I were driving home through the crisp fall air. We had the moonroof open so Jill could lean back and look up at the stars while I drove.

"Let's take Route 44," Jill said suddenly, flashing me a sideways look from her lovely green eyes.

"Hoping to see a ghost?" I chuckled, taking the turn as directed.

"Ha!" Jill snorted derisively. "As if! It's just quicker that way. I'm ready for bed!"

She yawned and stretched luxuriously, turning her head to face the passenger window as she did so. Suddenly, she let out a shriek of sheer terror. I jumped and glanced sideways, my hands shaking on the steering wheel from the unexpectedness of the sound. A red-haired man with a bushy beard wearing a plaid shirt and blue jeans was running right next to the passenger side of the car—I had already accelerated to nearly fifty mph after making the turn! He kept glancing in the window and leering at Jill. Through the open moonroof, we could hear the sound of manic laughter as the phantom kept pace with the speeding car.

"Oh my God, oh my God," Jill prayed desperately. "Jerry, get us out of here!"

Heart pounding in terror, I hit the gas. The car lurched and zoomed forward, leaving the phantom behind. Jill gasped and craned her head back to look at the figure. Then she

THE HITCHHIKER

screamed again, a terrible sound that made me swerve the car spasmodically. The tires screeched and the car tipped a bit. I fought to regain control, shouting: "What! What?" A moment later, I felt the car respond to my steering, and I pulled us back into our lane.

As soon as it was safe to do so, I glanced in the rearview mirror and saw the answer to my question. The red-haired man with the bushy beard was sitting in the back seat of our car. Jill shrieked again and lunged for her purse. Wheeling around as far as the seat belt would allow, she began pummeling the phantom with her purse, shouting: "Get out! Get out right now!"

I kept looking back and forth between my wife, the phantom, and the road ahead, determined that I was not going to let the red-haired ghost force us into a fatal accident.

Once I was sure the car was under control, I glanced toward the back seat and saw Jill's purse pass right through the man's head and out the other side of his glowing body. The ghost laughed again, a menacing laugh that made my teeth tingle and the hairs on my neck stand up.

"Hail Mary, full of grace; the Lord is with thee. Blessed art thou among women, and blessed is the fruit of thy womb, Jesus." Jill gabbled the words of the rosary, grabbing for the cross she always wore around her neck.

Glancing in the mirror, I saw the phantom grimace as she recited the holy words. Then he vanished without a trace.

"Get us out of here," Jill cried, throwing her purse into the back seat to make sure the phantom was gone. It hit the cushions with a thud.

I got us out of there much faster than the speed limit allowed. I was shaking from head to toe, and Jill was sobbing hysterically, tugging at her fingers one at a time in her agitation. As soon as I pulled into the driveway and turned off the car, I swept my wife into my arms and held her as tightly as I could. We clung together for a long time, until both of us had stopped shaking and Jill's sobs had abated.

"I want to go inside," Jill whispered against my neck, and I nodded, not trusting my voice. I retrieved her purse from the floor of the back seat, slipped out the driver's side, and helped her out. Keeping a tight grip on my precious wife, who had so valiantly fought the phantom of Route 44, I half-walked half-carried her into the house and ushered her straight upstairs and into our bed. When she was settled, I ran downstairs and made her a tray with hot cocoa and crackers—her favorite comfort food. While I was at it, I put another cup and plate on for myself, since I felt the need of some comfort as well.

We snuggled together in bed, sipping cocoa and discussing the terrifying incident. Then we fell asleep in each others arms. Oddly enough, neither of us had nightmares, and when we woke in the morning with the sun streaming in through the lacy curtains at our window, I felt much better about the whole thing. Until I remembered my promise to Sandy the night before. I groaned aloud and then clapped a hand over my mouth lest the sound wake my wife. Too late. She opened her green eyes and gave me a sleepy smile.

"Guess what?" she mumbled at me.

"What?" I mumbled back at her.

"You owe Sandy a year's worth of pizza," Jill said.

"I most certainly do," I replied, rubbing the back of her neck gently. "I most certainly do!"

10

Hide and Seek

Our friends invited us on a dinner cruise in their yacht to celebrate our twentieth anniversary. After dinner, they would drop us off at the Vineyard, where my husband had booked us into a nice inn for the weekend. The weather was overcast and windy when we set out just before dinner, but Steve—our host and captain—assured us that it would clear up soon. Right. Within the hour the heavens had opened and rain poured down upon us. The Bermuda-rigged sloop was tossed this way and that, and our dinner slid off our plates—which was okay by me because I was so seasick I couldn't eat. Given the choice of facing the terrible lurching below deck or the rain outside, I opted for outside. I grimly clung to the rail for the rest of the journey, shivering in the wind and rain and the occasional slap of a too-enthusiastic wave.

"Happy anniversary, honey," I growled sarcastically to my husband after depositing what was left of my dinner overboard.

"We're almost there," Thomas said soothingly, patting my back sympathetically.

We docked at the marina around nine o'clock. By the time

Thomas got us a taxi and we arrived at the inn, all I wanted was a hot shower and bed. What I did not want was a ghost. But that was exactly what I got as soon as I stepped foot in the renovated old tavern-turned-inn that was our home away from home for the weekend.

I've always had psychic tendencies and have been able to see ghosts since childhood. This is not a skill I discuss with most people, including Thomas. My husband—while tolerant of my "foible"—still thinks I am imagining the whole thing. When we first started dating, I told him I could sense ghosts, and he laughed at me and refused to believe. After that, I didn't dare tell him I could see them too. He'd never have understood. So as I stood wet and miserable in the entrance to the inn, watching him register, I decided not to mention the fact that his shoes were being carefully sniffed by a semitransparent ghost dog with a lashing tail and an engaging sparkle in its eyes. Anyway, I was too sick at the moment to care about the ghost dog, though normally I would have given such a happy creature a surreptitious pat when no one was looking.

My husband had booked something special for our anniversary, or so he claimed. He was beaming as he escorted me through a bookcase in the wall that masked a secret staircase leading to charming guestroom. The ghost dog accompanied us, and as soon as my feet touched the first step I knew that the poor old fellow had died here a long time ago.

What I didn't expect, as we set down our suitcases, was for two small heads to pop out through the wall, followed by two charming little ghost-boys who promptly slid under our bed, giggling at each other. The dog wiggled underneath too, and I saw the three of them peeping out at us while my husband started unpacking his things. I frowned at them ferociously. I was still feeling seriously seasick and was *not* in the mood for hide-and-seek.

I grabbed a robe and slippers and headed to the bathroom, calling: "I don't want any interruptions while I'm in the bath." At the door, I paused to glare first at my spouse and then at the bed where the boys lay hidden. They giggled, and one of them made a horrible face at me. Since Thomas had his back turned, I made a horrible face back, and they both laughed delightedly.

"Take your time," Thomas said, ignoring my grumpiness as he unfolded his pajamas. "And feel better."

"Harrumph!" I snorted as I left the four of them behind me for blessed hot water in an unmoving surface. When I returned to the bedroom, my husband was the only one in residence. Good. I crawled into bed and fell asleep right away.

In the morning, my crankiness and seasickness had both abated, to Thomas's and my relief, and we sat down to a fabulous breakfast. I was feeling downright perky by the time we were done and even stopped to pat the ghost-dog who accompanied us out into the bright, rain-washed summer morning, on the pretext of tying my shoe.

Thomas and I strolled around town like a couple of courting teenagers, laughing and holding hands. We peeked into the quaint shops, and I talked Thomas out of buying a scrimshaw for our house. We rented bicycles and rode all over the island. By day's end, we were sunburnt and happily exhausted. Back at the inn, we climbed the secret staircase in the old tavern wall, and I waved to the little ghost boy who was hiding behind the door.

After dinner, I wandered downstairs without my disbelieving spouse and casually asked a member of the waitstaff at the

HIDE AND SEEK

restaurant if the house was haunted. I prompted him a bit by mentioning that we were spending the weekend in the secret room behind the bookcase.

"Oh, are you staying there?" he asked brightly. "There *is* a ghost story associated with that room."

I settled myself down to listen as he related the following tale. Back in the 1800s, the old tavern had been converted into a residence, and a couple lived here with their two little boys and a small dog, who was the pride and joy of their younger son. The older boy was a bit of a prankster, and one evening before leaving for an extended stay with his grandmother, he shut the dog into the secret room to tease his little brother. Well, the young chap went searching for his dog, not hearing the whining and scratching behind the wall, and ended up racing out into a rainstorm. The younger brother came down with pneumonia the next day and died soon after without ever knowing where his dog had been hidden. It was only after the funeral that the poor little dog was found in the secret room, where he'd died from thirst and starvation. When the older boy returned home from his lengthy visit and learned the consequences of his prank, he threw himself into the harbor and drowned.

Tears sprang to my eyes at the close of the tragic story, and I didn't need the young man to tell me that the brothers and their little dog were rumored to haunt the inn.

"Some people have heard the brothers giggling, and others have seen paw prints on the floor," he concluded. "Especially in the secret room. Sometimes we leave biscuits out for the dog."

"And I'm sure he appreciates them," I said, watching the bright-eyed ghost-dog sitting just behind him, tail lashing in delight.

After thanking the boy, I headed back to the room, accompanied by the ghostly dog, who bumped into (and through) my legs.

"The wind's a bit strong tonight," Thomas commented, looking up from his book as I entered. "I keep hearing it muttering around the corners of the house. Sounds a bit like someone chuckling."

"Or two someones," I agreed, watching one of the boys hide Thomas's slippers under the dresser. The ghost-boy caught my eye and giggled, and suddenly my eyes were covered from behind by a small pair of cold hands. I heard a soft giggle right in my ear. Then both boys vanished, and the dog disappeared a moment later—all but his tail, which wagged several times and then slowly faded away. I blinked a few times and then my eyes focused on Thomas. He was staring at me with an arrested look on his face.

"You know, I could almost swear I saw a little boy standing behind you," he said in a faraway voice. The newspaper in his hands rattled, and I realized he was shaking. "But he's not there anymore."

"Just a ghost, dear. Don't let it worry you," I said in a soothing voice.

Thomas swallowed hard and then said: "I think it best if I pretend that nothing just happened." He ducked back behind his newspaper, and I heard him give a shuddering sigh.

"You do that, dear," I said, and winked as a little head popped out from under his chair. The younger brother tried to wink back, but he'd obviously never learned how, so it turned into more of an eyelash flutter.

We had a lovely weekend at the inn, and I was sad to say goodbye to the happy ghosts who inhabited the secret room behind the bookcase.

"We'll come back again," said Thomas as we carried our luggage outside to our taxi. But looking back, I sensed that this was the last time we would visit this particular spot. And I was right. Our travels have taken us many places in the decades since then, but we've never been back to the Vineyard.

11

Lovers' Tryst

SOMERVILLE

Her old man was against the match. That was the crux of the matter. The old man had money and wanted his daughter to marry well. Instead, she had fallen for him—a simple farm-boy who lived down the road.

He'd been surprised when he first caught her eyeing him at school and then shyly pleased to discover they shared a sense of humor and a deep love of nature and the wild things that inhabited their world. They'd sometimes meet in the fields while she was out walking, and he noticed that this began to happen too many times to be a coincidence.

By the time they'd been "accidently" meeting for six months, he was head over heels in love. Shortly after he realized this, he proposed and she accepted. They weren't sure how to approach her father with the news and spent quite a bit of time discussing it. It was late autumn and too cold to go out walking, so instead they started meeting each evening at the abandoned windmill, where they would sit and talk for hours. He wanted to be married right away, but she wanted a spring wedding. She also thought it would take her six months or more to talk her father into the match.

They had just reached this point in their nightly discussion when he glanced out the window and saw a tall figure striding purposefully down the lane. Her father! His weathered face wore a thunderous frown, and he was carrying a heavy walking stick in his hands.

His betrothed gasped in alarm when she saw her father's approach. "Hide!" she told him urgently. "Quickly. Behind the door."

"There's not room for two of us," he whispered.

"I'll hide in the loft," she said, and hurried toward the steps. The last flounces of her dress were just disappearing over the edge of the loft when the door flew open—almost hitting him in the nose—and her father walked in, slapping his walking stick to and fro. The mill was dark, and the old man had brought no lantern in his haste to disrupt the lovers' tryst. The old man groped about in the dark, cursing aloud as he searched for his erring daughter and her swain.

Swallowing hard, the boy backed even further behind the open door, and overhead he heard the soft shuffle of footsteps as his betrothed edged further back herself. Then he heard her stumble and give a muffled cry. A rope jerked near his ear as his betrothed caught hold of it to save herself from a fall. The tug on the rope triggered the windmill fans, which suddenly began to whir and clank.

"Ah, ha!" he heard the old man shout. The shout was followed by a gasp, a thud, and then a scream of agony. The young farmer immediately leapt from his hiding place and ran toward the sound. He heard his betrothed racing down the stairs from the loft as he reached her father's side. The old man had been standing on a millstone when the sails of the windmill began to turn. He'd lost his balance when the stone started to move and had fallen, his arm landing between the two grinding surfaces. In the faint light filtering through the window, the young farmer could see that the old man's arm was crushed and that blood was seeping everywhere.

Instructing his betrothed to hold her father still, he stopped the sails and then gently pulled the old man out. The young farmer tenderly wrapped the remains of the bloody pulp that was the old man's arm into his coat and carried him home, even remembering to bring the walking stick with which the old man had intended to beat him.

The old man soon lost consciousness, which was a mercy. There was nothing they could do to save his arm, though the doctor did everything possible. The daughter nursed her father faithfully in the weeks following the accident, but he never really recovered from the shock and died two months later. On his last night on earth, the old man summoned the young farmer to him and gruffly told him to marry his daughter and keep her out of trouble. With those parting words, he breathed his last.

His betrothed flung herself down beside the bed, weeping copiously, and he gathered her up in his arms. For a moment she resisted his embrace, and the young farmer thought she was going to repudiate him as a penance, since she was the one who had accidentally started the windmill fans that had crushed her father's arm. Then she broke down, allowing him to hold her and comfort her as best he could.

They were married very quietly a few weeks later, as befitted a house of mourning, and his new wife moved out to the farm with him. She was happy overall, he could tell, but she would never go near the old windmill, and the shadow of her father's death lay over her heart.

It didn't help the situation when some of the villagers who lived near the windmill started seeing the old man's ghost haunting the mill on windy nights. They claimed he stomped up and down inside the dark, ramshackle building, waving his cane and swearing so loudly that blue lights danced around his head.

When the young farmer's wife first heard this rumor, she turned pale and almost fainted. Her husband glared at the neighbor-woman who had brought the news, and she hastily made her excuses and left their house. But the damage was done. His wife stood by the window, wringing her hands until he gently took them into his own.

"Your father didn't blame you," he said gently. "It was an accident."

"I as good as killed him," his wife cried, tears rolling down his cheeks. "If I had told him about our courtship, he never would have come to the mill. If I hadn't insisted on hiding, I wouldn't have stumbled and started the fans turning."

"If your father had been less proud about his money and status, if he had waited to confront you when you came home, none of this would have happened either," the young man exclaimed. But she was beyond reason.

He knew, of course, what she would do. The next windy night, she slipped out of their bed, threw on her shawl, and headed for the old windmill. He followed her, catching up with her in the lane and silently taking hold of her hand. She tried to pull away, but he kept a tight hold on her. After a moment, he felt her relax and accept his presence. They had started this together, and they would end it together, for better or for worse.

Though neither spoke a word, he knew they were in agreement about this.

They could hear the ghost of the old man as soon as they turned down the overgrown lane that led to the abandoned mill. He was swearing up a storm, as he had on the night of the accident, and they could hear the swish, swish of his cane as he whipped it hither and thither.

Squaring his shoulders, the young farmer opened the door to the mill and stepped inside, his wife hard on his heels. Balancing on top of the millstone stood his dead father-in-law, blue lights dancing about his glowing, one-armed form.

"Ah, ha!" the phantom shouted when he saw the young farmer. "Courting my only daughter, eh? Trying to get ahold of my money!"

"No, sir," the young farmer replied. "I never wanted your money. I just love your daughter and want her for my wife." He swallowed heavily, remembering the words he had rehearsed so many times during their stealthy courtship.

The phantom swooped down from the millstone and hovered above him. They were so close their noses almost touched, and the chill from the phantom flesh made shivers run through his whole body. It took great presence of mind to keep him from shrinking backward from the ghost.

After a moment, the old man straightened up, pleased by what he saw in the young farmer's eyes. "Well, I approve," he roared, waving the walking stick above his head. "Not many men would face down a phantom to get their woman. Take her with my blessing."

This was too much for his daughter. She sprang forward and dropped to her knees below the one-armed ghost. "Father, I'm

LOVERS' TRYST

sorry! I'm sorry! Forgive me!" She writhed on the dusty floor, huge tears falling from her eyes.

The phantom was embarrassed. Glancing sheepishly at his son-in-law, he floated down to the floor and patted her on the shoulder. "There, there, lass. T'accident was my own fault, anyhow. I shouldn't have come stalking you at the mill. There was plenty of time to talk about your young man when you got home that night. Don't cry."

His daughter's tears slowly dried, and gradually she sat up within the circle of the phantom arm. The ghost gave her a brief kiss on the cheek and said: "Go to your husband now, there's a good lass. And don't forget I want lots of grandchildren. You two better get crackin'!"

The old man's ghost floated up toward the millstone, and he grinned down at his son-in-law, who bent to help his wife to her feet.

"God bless you both," he said suddenly, and vanished with a popping sound. Immediately, the mill was plunged into darkness, and the young farmer heard his wife gasp. He held her close to his heart while his eyes adjusted to the gloom and then helped her outside. They walked home hand in hand, at peace together for the first time since the old man's accident.

"And don't forget," he whispered in her ear as they entered their house, "we've got to get cracking on those grandchildren!"

His wife giggled, pecked him on the cheek, and then went running for the stairs leading up to their second-story bedroom. With a laugh of sheer relief, the young farmer followed her upstairs.

12

The Fireside Chair

SALEM

For some reason, he was thinking about ghosts as he left his tall, many-gabled house to do some research at the library. He was an aspiring writer, and he liked to spend his free hours working in the members-only reading room. He had been delayed this morning by a last-minute task and was impatient to get to the Athenaeum. As he hurried through the streets, his thoughts turned to the supernatural, as they often did these days.

He had been surrounded by ghost stories all his life, though he was not sure if he really believed them. Still, if anyplace in the world was haunted, it would be this town called Salem, with its violent history. The Salem witch trials of 1692 had created so many supposed hauntings they could hardly be counted. His own home was supposed to house the ghost of a dressmaker, whom his cousin Susan once claimed to have seen sewing by the window.

Then, the writer mused, there was the curse of old Giles Corey, accused warlock. When Corley refused to stand trial for practicing black magic, High Sheriff Corwin—an evil and greedy man who sent many an innocent person to the gallows and then claimed their property as his own—resurrected an ancient English law that allowed accused witches and warlocks to be crushed under heavy stones if they did not stand trial. Corwin had stripped the old man naked, put him in a pit in an open field with a board on top of his body, and then proceed to place large boulders on top of him, trying to "crush the truth" out of him. It didn't work. At the last, the words that sprang from Corey's mouth were those of a curse against the sheriff and against Salem itself. It seemed to have worked. The sheriff died of a heart attack a few years later, as had many of his successors. And Corey's ghost was said to haunt the local graveyard, often appearing just before a calamity.

These were the writer's musings as he dodged a mud-spattered carriage and entered the building that housed the subscription library. Quietly, he removed hat and cloak and made his way to his favorite seat in the reading room, nodding to various acquaintances as he passed. He noted absently that the white-haired, rather infirm Reverend Harris had claimed his favorite seat by the fireplace and was intently studying the *Boston Post*, as was his custom each day. He caught the old man's eye and nodded politely. The minister stared back rather longer than politeness allowed, and through the next several hours, the writer looked up to find Harris's gaze upon him more than once. It made him feel uncomfortable, but he ignored it in favor of the journals he was studying.

The writer went to a restaurant for dinner that evening, and while there a friend told him that the good minister Harris had passed to his reward that very day. The writer was shocked, having just seen the man a few hours before in the reading room. After a moment's reflection, he decided the old man must have died after leaving the library. Still, it was surprising that the word had

THE FIRESIDE CHAIR

gotten around so fast. Throughout the evening, other friends and acquaintances confirmed the sad event, and the writer felt a pang as he realized he would never again see the minister sitting in the fireside chair at the library.

The thought remained with him the next day as he entered the Athenaeum and walked to his favorite place in the reading room. The writer was just settling himself down to the day's research when he glanced toward the fireplace and saw Reverend Harris sitting in his favorite chair, perusing the *Boston Post*. The writer stared in amazement at the deceased minister, wondering if the story of his death had been an elaborate joke played on him by his friends. Then he realized he could see—very faintly—the back of the chair through the old man's body. He *was* a ghost!

Throughout the afternoon, the writer surreptitiously watched the minister as he read his way through the newspaper. No one else in the room appeared to notice the specter, and the writer was afraid to draw attention to it lest the others think he had gone mad. Once, the dead minister looked up from his paper and nodded at the writer. Cautiously, he nodded back. What a bizarre situation to be in, he mused, trying to concentrate on his studies. But the phantom drew his eye again and again, until he was forced to abandon his work and go home for the evening.

Every day for several weeks, the writer encountered the phantom in the reading room. They never spoke, but sometimes he felt the minister's gaze upon him as he studied or wrote in his notebooks. No one else in the subscription library mentioned the phantom, though the writer noticed that no one ever tried to claim the prized chair by the fire.

After the first several days, the shock of the ghost's appearance wore off, and the writer came to accept him as a natural part of the club atmosphere. Which was why he felt another shock the day he entered the room and found the fireside chair empty. His hands shook as he gathered the day's materials and went to sit in his favorite spot. First the ghost was here, and then it was gone. What meaning could it have? He would probably never know, he mused to himself.

As the writer turned back to his papers, he felt an idea stirring. In his mind's eye he saw a house with seven gables, built upon the property of a condemned wizard by the man who helped bring him to the scaffold. It was a haunted house. Haunted by the memory (or perhaps even the noncorporeal reality?) of the dead wizard. There would be a curse, too. Yes, a curse uttered at the moment of the wizard's death. The writer smiled to himself, glanced over at the fireside chair, now devoid of its phantom, and jotted his idea down in a notebook.

A few minutes later, when a club member wandered over to the fireplace and sat in the empty chair, the writer didn't even feel a pang. Somehow, he knew that the minister had—at last—gone to his just reward.

PART TWO
Powers of Darkness and Light

13

Madness

SALEM

I watch in silent glee as the first seeds of madness are scattered onto the fertile ground of this place called Salem . . .

It begins in 1689, when the new minister, Samuel Parris, moves into Salem Village with his family. They own a slave woman named Tituba. I study the slave with interest, for the secret tenets of her religion are dark indeed, and she believes them utterly. It is she who—unbeknownst—begins planting the seeds of destruction as she relates the stories of her people to the young ones. Such a small thing, and yet it will grow into a terrible storm come the spring of 1692.

I introduce myself immediately to the family, and soon I am considered a dear friend and an excellent Christian. Oh, yes, I chuckle inwardly, I am indeed an excellent Christian— outwardly! Soon I am taking tea with the minister's wife once a week, sitting before the fire and discussing church work. And quietly, I nurture the seeds of madness and watch them grow within the household.

In January of 1692, I make my customary visit to the minister's house for tea and talk. It is a fine winter day, and I sit sipping from my cup and watching little Betty Parris playing near the hearth. She drops her ball and it rolls into the hearth—too close to the fire. She stretches out her hand to retrieve it, and I say softly: "I wouldn't if I were you, my dear."

I tug on the handkerchief in my lap, pulling it toward me to cover the small gesture I make with my hidden hand. In front of me, little Betty's hand stops abruptly a few inches from the hot fire. She cries out in surprise, causing her mother to look over to see what is wrong. Seeing how close the child is to the fire, her mother gasps and pulls little Betty away from the hearth, sending her to the kitchen to sit with Tituba. I watch the little girl leave with a slight smile on my lips. I do not wish this particular child to be damaged in any way. No indeed. For I have looked into her eyes and seen the madness that has taken hold of her soul.

Just a few days later, Elizabeth comes to me with a frightened face and a disturbing story. Little Betty has been stricken with terrible convulsions, dashing about, diving under furniture, contorting in pain, and complaining of fever. The child had even screamed blasphemous words in the midst of her madness.

I am suitably shocked and take care not to speak of witchcraft. It is too soon to speak of this to Elizabeth Parris. But I drop hints to the other good folk in the village, priming the pump so that the madness will come gushing forth.

I possess a copy of that very useful book penned by Cotton Mather. It is called *Memorable Providences* and describes the suspected witchcraft of an Irish washerwoman in Boston. In a careful and discreet way, I bring the villager's attention to the close parallel between Betty's behavior and that of the witchcraft victim described in the book. It goes down very well, and it is not long before the doctor himself believes the child is bewitched.

Soon, Little Betty's bizarre behavior spreads to encompass eleven-year-old Abigail Williams, Ann Putnam Jr., and other Salem girls. The girls contort into grotesque poses, fall down in frozen postures, and complain of biting and pinching sensations. "Witchcraft," some whisper. It does not take long for this rumor to spread. In just a few days, the populace is shouting the words aloud in the street: "The girls are bewitched."

I mention casually to Mistress Sibley, a neighbor of the afflicted family, that something must be done to counter the enchantment. My hint is enough. Soon she conspires with Tituba to bake a rye cake made with the urine of the afflicted child and feed it to a dog, an old folk cure sure to help the girl. This un-Christian response to the problem focuses community attention on the slave woman who believes so strongly in the supernatural. Perhaps she is the answer to their problem.

Two days after the rye cake is baked, arrest warrants are issued against Tituba; Sarah Good, a social misfit; and Sarah Osborn, who has not attended church for a year. Two of the afflicted children—Betty Parris and Abigail Williams—name these three women as the source of their troubles, and they are believed.

The Putnam family, whose daughter Ann is among the afflicted seven, bring a complaint against the three women to county magistrates Jonathan Corwin and John Hathorne, who schedule examinations for the suspected witches on March 1, 1692, in Ingersoll's tavern.

On the day of the examination, hundreds of people arrive to watch the show. (Oh, dear, a slip of the tongue. I mean *the trial.*) The examinations are moved to the meeting house, where the girls describe the attacks made on them by the specters of the three women. When approached by the accused, the girls fall into contortions. Other villagers come forward with tales of deformed animals and the *highly suspicious* circumstance of butter and cheese gone bad after a visit by one or another of the women. The magistrates speak to the women, hammering them over and over with the same questions: Are you witches? Have you seen Satan? How, if you are not witches, do you explain the contortions caused by your presence? I am delighted by the performance. It is obvious that the magistrates think the women guilty as charged.

But it has not gone far enough for me. Not yet. The magistrates seem set on admonishing the women and letting them go. This will not do. I roll my handkerchief into a ball as I place a picture into the mind of Tituba. She is impressionable and breaks easily. A moment later, she tells the magistrates that she was once approached by a tall dark man who asked her to sign his book and do his work. The commotion this confession causes among the crowd is delightful to hear.

Soon Tituba gives way to lofty flights of imagination, claiming to fly through the air in the company of four other witches and claiming that the Devil blocked her whenever she tried to confess and repent of her sins to the good Reverend Parris. Her confession is the spark that sets the village aflame. Soon, the local ministers are hunting for witches and finding them everywhere.

The night after the first trial, I spend an hour drawing the face of a village woman upon the bark of a tree. It is a good likeness of the woman, whom I hate. Rebecca Nurse slighted me many years ago, and I have never forgotten it or forgiven her. Now I take the picture and drop it into the stream, where the water will eat away at it until it is gone—and Rebecca Nurse with it.

Drunk with their newly perceived power, the "bewitched" girls start accusing more women of witchcraft. Their writhing antics are believed and more arrests ensue, including those of Martha Corey and Rebecca Nurse. One Sunday during church service, Ann Putnam suddenly shouts: "Look where Goodwife Cloyce sits on the beam suckling her yellow bird between her fingers!" This is taken as proof of Sarah Cloyce's guilt by many who hear the child's words. The girls even accuse the four-year-old daughter of Sarah Good of sending a specter to bite them. A foul accusation indeed, and even I am shocked when the child is arrested and put into prison. After all, we must preserve the future generation, or who will be left for us to dominate? I set a spell that night to make sure the girls will send no more children to prison.

The jails are filling up rapidly with accused witches, much to the delight of the girls and also, I see, local Sheriff Corwin, who is not above skimming a profit off the proceedings. Interesting.

The girls have enhanced their performances by this time. Sometimes, they pretend to be struck dumb by the witches who are tormenting them. Other times, they scream and writhe in agony and pretend to see visions. They are widely believed, and other villages send for the girls to discover if they too are plagued by witches. Strangely, all of them are—according to the little dears.

Some of the accused begin to "confess" to their crimes, fearing the gallows. This increases the fear and tension in all the towns surrounding Salem. By the time newly appointed Governor Phipps arrives from England, the jails are full, and the colony is in chaos.

Phipps creates a new court, the "court of oyer and terminer," to try the witchcraft cases, and he appoints to it five judges, including, I note, three close friends of Cotton Mather. At Mather's urging, the court admits spectral evidence, which is the testimony of the afflicted who claim to see the apparition or the shape of the person afflicting them. They also instigate the touch test, in which the accused are asked to touch the victims, it being assumed that the touch of a witch will stop the contortions of the afflicted. The court even had the accused examined for "witch marks"—moles thought to be created by the bite of a witch's familiar. Hearsay, gossip, unsupported assertions, surmises—all these and more become evidence against the accused, who are given no legal counsel, can have no witnesses testify on their behalf, and who are not allowed to appeal a verdict.

Bridget Bishop, owner of a tavern, is the first brought to trial on June 2, 1692. She is also the first to die. Following her hanging, Justice Nathaniel Saltonstall resigns from the court in disgust, but I am relieved to see that this does not deter the bloodlust of the other justices, and Bridget Bishop's death is rapidly followed by others.

I wait impatiently for accusations to be made against Rebecca Nurse and finally push a vision of her into the minds of several of the afflicted girls. The next day, Rebecca Nurse is named a witch, and a trial follows shortly. To my surprise, both Ann Putnam Jr. *and* Ann Putnam Sr. accuse her of witchcraft. No one heeds the fact that Nurse is a member of a Topsfield family that has had a long-standing quarrel with the Putnams.

To my fury, the Nurse jury returns a verdict of not guilty. But a few twists of my handkerchief turn the mind of Chief Justice

Stoughton, who tells the jury to reconsider a statement of Nurse's that he considers an admission of guilt. The jury reconvenes and brings back a verdict of guilty. On July 19, 1692, Nurse rides with four other convicted witches to Gallows Hill.

The following week is enlivened by yet more histrionics by the girls. They writhe and contort, and little Betty Parris's eyes dart to and fro, seeking another victim. For a moment they land on me, gleaming. Calmly, I smile at her, and into her mind I say: "I wouldn't if I were you, my dear." Betty's eyes widen in shock and she screams in real agony as I give a small twist to the handkerchief in my lap, and red welts form upon her neck and face. She cowers back, her eyes sliding frantically from side to side. They land upon a woman in the next pew, a woman who had been on the opposite side of her father in a recent congregational dispute, and little Betty screams her name aloud, pointing her free hand at the newly accused witch. "Good girl," I whisper into her mind, releasing the handkerchief and with it my spell. The red welts fade from her skin as if they had never been. I find it strange, as I watch Betty writhe on the meeting room floor, screaming the names of her tormentors, that the people of Salem see the Devil's handiwork everywhere but in the one place where it is most visible.

As the summer progresses, those who have scoffed at the trials, such as tavern owner John Proctor, become targets of the accusers. Ex-minister George Burroughs is dragged back from his home in Maine to face trial after Ann Putnam claims that he bewitched soldiers during a failed military campaign in the frontier war. Mercy Lewis tells the court that Burroughs flew her to the top of a mountain and, pointing toward the surrounding land, promised her all the kingdoms if only she would sign his book. When he is executed, Burroughs not only refuses to confess, but he recites the Lord's Prayer perfectly, something that the Colony believes cannot be done by a witch. (How wrong they are!) The crowd is greatly moved, but the execution goes forward at Cotton Mather's behest.

I find it amazing that no one seems to notice that most of the accused are better off financially than the accusers, and that many of the accusing families stand to gain property from the convictions of accused witches. And of course, many of the accusers sided against George Burroughs in the schism that split the church a few years back. But the witch-hysteria is so strong now that practical matters are brushed aside in favor of specters and bad luck and fanciful stories. And Sheriff Corwin collects fees, confiscates property, and delights in his power over his neighbors almost as much as the "afflicted" girls and their families.

One of the accused, an eighty-year-old man named Giles Corey, sees through the façade. Understanding the futility of a trial and knowing that the state will seize his farm if he is convicted of witchcraft, Corey remains mute when asked to lodge a plea with the court, hoping to preserve the family farm for his sons-in-law. The English penalty for such a refusal was *peine et fort*—death by pressing. It is torture—plain and simple—and involves piling heavy stones on top of the victim until the truth is "pressed" out of him (or he dies.)

Corey is condemned to death. On September 19, he is stripped naked, pushed into a pit dug in the field behind the Salem jail, and his body pressed underneath heavy stones. Sheriff Corwin hangs over the pit, asking over and over for the old man to confess. Corey says nothing, though more and more stones are piled upon him, making his eyes bulge and his tongue pop out of his mouth. Corwin pushes the tongue back in and keeps piling on stones. Corey dies two days later, cursing the Sheriff and Salem with his last breath.

The whole town is shocked and subdued by the torture undergone by the old man. And still, the witch trials continue. Three days after Corey's death, on September 22, 1692, eight more convicted witches, including Corey's wife, are hanged.

It cannot last, of course. The Reverend John Hale begins to question the probability of so many prominent citizens embracing the Devil's work all at once, and even the foolish concede his point. Yet as I look at the greedy, gullible, vain faces of the accusing girls and their kinfolk, I believe the good reverend is wrong. It is possible for a large number of people to simultaneously embrace the Devil. In Salem, we called them the accusers.

Then Increase Mather—father of devoted witch-hunter Cotton Mather—prints a tract arguing that it is better to let suspected witches escape than kill the innocent. And—to my chagrin—a Bostonian minister named Samuel Willard writes another suggesting that the Devil himself might create the specter of an innocent person and parade it before the eyes of the afflicted. (A fact I would rather not have gotten out, since I myself had used this trick more than once.)

The opinions of these men sway the heart of the governor, who orders the court to exclude spectral evidence and touching tests. Without these, the trials are proved a sham. The girls continue with their accusations for a few months more, but reach too high when they accuse the governor's own wife of being a witch. Within a month of this accusation, the trials are

MADNESS

shut down, and all accused witches are released from jail. And so the madness dies away at last, and the witch trials come to a bitter conclusion. According to my private records, nineteen convicted witches have been executed, four have died in prison, Giles Corey has been pressed to death, and between one to two hundred other people have been arrested and imprisoned on charges of witchcraft.

Life slowly returns to normal in Salem. Every Sabbath, I walk silently through the churchyard, carrying my prayer book. Around me, the congregants are sober and exhausted, glad to see an end to the madness. I am sated for the moment by all the bloodshed and pain and anguish, but it will not be long before I crave more. I walk down the aisle and take my seat. Laying my prayer book in my lap, I piously turn my attention toward the altar where the minister calls us to worship. For countless generations, all the women in my family have been witches. And none of us have ever been caught.

14

The Wise-Woman and the Witch

GLOUCESTER

Johnny was lost at sea. I knew it, deep within my soul, and it made my heart wring with pain. His ship had been gone ten months—ten months!—and there had come no word from them at all after the first two. The winter storms had arrived—such terrible storms. How could a ship survive? My betrothed was missing, perhaps dead, and I was in despair.

My parents tried to laugh me out of my heaviness. Merchant ships were often gone two or three years at a time, my father said, patting my cheek as he rose from the breakfast table. Johnny hadn't even been gone a year, Mama added, as she cleared away the dishes. But my heart was heavy. I moped about the house and lost weight and stared day after day out to sea, hoping against hope that my Johnny would return.

It seemed to me that I had always loved Johnny, my handsome next-door neighbor. I followed him around as a child, worshipped the ground he walked on as an awkward schoolgirl, and had been swept off my feet by him as a young woman. We were made for one another. That was what everyone said. A perfect match. But now he was gone—ten months gone—and my greatest fear was that I would never see my wonderful sailor-man again.

It was my mother who finally took me in hand. One morning, after my strict church-going father had left for work in the local sawmill, she took me aside, scolded me for my lack of faith, and then said: "Grace, they say that old Goody Hascall is a wise-woman. She always seems to know when a sailor or ship will not come home, and she has never been wrong. I know your father does not approve of scrying, but I would advise you to speak to her, to set your mind at ease." Then she kissed the top of my head and left me to think it over.

My heart was pounding madly in my chest as I watched her walk down the stairs toward the front parlor. Goody Haskell lived in a small clearing with her sister Jezebel. Folks around here called the two sisters "the wise-woman and the witch." Hannah Haskell was a skilled herbalist and midwife who delivered all the local babies and aided the sick more effectively than the local doctor. But Jezebel, with her wild eyes and her wild hair, was an object of fear. It was rumored that she had dealings with Satan and was the leader of a coven of witches who hexed farms, made good people go mad, and sold love potions and other more sinister concoctions to the desperate. She could change herself into a black cat and spy on people—at least, that's what my friends said. I didn't mind talking to Hannah Haskell, but to do so meant possibly meeting Jezebel at the little house in the clearing. I wasn't sure what to do.

That night, a great storm blew in from the sea, and for the next several days it raged on and on. On the third day it cleared, and I heard my parents talking anxiously in soft voices when I came down the stairs for breakfast. The look on their faces took my breath away, and the look on mine caused Mother to spring up in alarm and Father to say: "It's not about Johnny. There is still no word from the *Good Hope*." I sagged a little with relief, for as Mother said, in such cases, no news is good news. Then I straightened up. "What is it, then?"

Father looked grave. "The *Free Spirit* went down in the storm last night. All hands were lost."

I gasped and sank into a chair. Johnny's brother had been on the *Free Spirit*. I started trembling from head to toe, and Mother pulled me into her arms and soothed me as best she could. I struggled free then, saying: "I must go to Johnny's mother." Mentally, I added: "And I must see Goody Haskell."

I spent the day comforting the woman who might—if Johnny came home—be my mother-in-law. The next day, gathering my courage and praying that Jezebel would be out gathering herbs when I arrived, I set out for the tiny clearing in the woods where the wise-woman and the witch lived.

The day was dark and overcast, and the road muddy. My skirt was stained a good six inches up from the hem by the time I made my way to the neat little cottage set deep in the woods. It was surrounded by a white picket fence that Hannah Haskell kept in good repair, and there was a nice little vegetable and herb garden off to one side. I glimpsed a few gnarled apple trees at the back as I made my way trembling to the door. My knock was so light that it could barely be heard. I would have to do better than that, I thought, trying to take myself in hand.

I raised my fist to knock again, but at that moment the door was yanked opened by Jezebel Haskell, the wild-haired, yellow-eyed sister who frightened me so much. The suddenness of her appearance caught me off guard. I gaped at her, speechless with fear and astonishment.

Jezebel took one look at my pale, wan face and began to cackle like a fiend. "Come about your sailor boy?" she cried at once before I opened my mouth. "Afraid he is drowned, are you? Can you picture him sinking into the waves, gasping for breath, water filling his lungs, choking him, pulling him down as seaweed caresses his poor dead body?"

I gasped desperately, seeing it all as clearly as she described it. Johnny drowning. Johnny dead.

"Stop that, Jezebel," scolded a clear, sane voice that snapped me out of my gruesome musings. "Leave the poor girl alone. She just lost Johnny's brother to the sea. It is an honest question."

I looked past Jezebel into the room and met the kind eyes of Hannah Haskell. The wise-woman was as plain-faced and plump a woman as ever lived, but she had a quick mind and a kind heart. Everyone loved her. She came to me, took my shaking hand, and drew me to a sunny little table in the corner. A moment later, Jezebel banged a cup of steaming tea in front of me, looking grumpy.

"If you won't let me have a little fun with her, then I may as well go gather some herbs," she growled to her sister.

"Away with thee then," Hannah Haskell said, flapping a hand fondly at her. The wild-eyed witch gave me a nasty glare and stomped outside.

"My dear Grace," Hannah said when she was gone. "I have looked and Jezebel has looked, and neither of us can see Johnny's fate. It is completely unknown."

I swallowed heavily and put the steaming cup of tea back in the saucer without taking a sip. Some of the tea sloshed over the rim and burnt my hand, but I barely noticed.

"I have no hope," I whispered, staring down at the cup.

Hannah gently wiped the tea from my hand, and at her touch, the sting of the burn faded away.

Her look was kind and sincere. "There is only one thing I can suggest to help you," she said slowly, "if you have the strength to bear it. Not many do, and so I have hesitated to mention it to all but the most despairing and desperate."

I blinked, and felt a faint stirring of hope in my midsection: "What is it?" I asked eagerly, sitting up straight in my chair.

"There is a place not far from here—a place known only to the very wise—where twice a year, at midnight on the summer and winter solstice, a roll is called out on the wind by a voice not of this world," Hannah said slowly. "Some say it is called out by an angel, some a devil. Whichever it is, I have never known it to be wrong. The roll call is a list of all the sailors who have been claimed by the sea since the last solstice."

My heart was beating very fast now.

"Johnny?" I whispered.

Hannah shook her head. "At the winter solstice, I did not hear Johnny's name. So he was safe at that time. If you have the courage, you may come with me to that place at the summer solstice—which is tomorrow night—and listen for his name. If you hear it, he is dead. If not, he may still return to you."

My mouth was so dry I had to swallow twice before I could speak. "I will come," I said huskily. Hannah nodded and told me where to meet her. She warned me that I would have to be blindfolded and led part of the way, since it was a sacred place. I nodded my understanding. I didn't care. I would do anything, go anywhere to find out if my Johnny was all right.

When I left the house of the wise-woman, an owl followed me part of the way home. It was unusual to see such a bird abroad in daylight, and when I turned to look at it, the owl winked at me and let out the cackling laugh of a fiend. I gasped and took to my heels, followed for a long time by the sound of that laugh.

I slipped out of my bed the following night after my parents retired, wrapped myself in a shawl, and hurried out of town toward the clearing where the witch and the wise-woman lived. The moon was full so I needed no lantern as I made my way to the path through the forest. As I rounded the last bend, I was startled by a looming, wild-eyed figure standing in the path, wings flapping in the breeze. I let out a small shriek of fright and then recognized the witch Jezebel, wrapped in a flapping cloak, waiting for me beside her sister Hannah.

"Frightened, my dear? You should be," cackled Jezebel. In the light of the lantern, her eyes glowed like those of a demon.

"Hush, Jezebel," Hannah Haskell said, nudging her sister with her elbow.

"I am sorry, my dear," she continued, speaking to me, "but we will need to blindfold you now."

I nodded obediently and then started as Jezebel's hands appeared from behind me, pulling a large handkerchief down over my eyes. In a moment, the lantern light disappeared, and I felt the wise-woman and the witch each take one of my arms.

The next hour was a nightmare of stumbling blindly down many strange paths, guided gently on one side by Hannah and yanked roughly on the other by Jezebel. I had no idea if we were traveling in circles to confuse me or if the place we were going really was an hour away from the cottage. I only know that when the blindfold was removed, I stood on a moonlit beach next to a ruined watchtower, and that the ocean waves were falling

THE WISE-WOMAN AND THE WITCH

one over the other as they swept ashore. A silvery moonlit path streamed out across the water from the far horizon, and the chilly wind whipped against my face. I pulled the shawl tight around me and looked mutely at Hannah, wondering what I should do.

Jezebel was already clambering inside the ruins of the watchtower. "Come, girl," she snapped. "Sit still with us, and listen." Hannah nodded for me to follow the witch, and so I gingerly climbed over the rotted doorsill, dodged some fallen timber, and untangled my dress from a stray nail before sitting down beside her as directed. The wise-woman was at my heels, and she sat on the other side of me.

We waited in silence, and I watched the moonlit shadows dancing on the ruined walls. Light streamed through several gaps, and I saw that both Hannah and Jezebel were sitting with their eyes closed and their hands busily working, but what spell they wove I do not know. It was at that moment that I heard it. Soft as a whisper, a voice spoke from the top of the ruined watchtower. "Geoffrey Downs, Kenneth Platte, Stephen Larson," it began. "Lost from the brig *Mariner's Delight*."

The voice grew louder, gaining strength and taking on strange overtones that made my hair stand on end. "Etienne Dubois, Jean-Claude Blanc, Henri Baptiste . . . " One by one, the names rolled out above our heads, the voice continuing to grow until the thunder of it shook the walls of the watchtower. Dust shook down from loosened boards, and at the height of the roll call, a section of wall caved in, revealing the moon-swept ocean waves and letting in the wind.

I shivered and shook and kept my hands clapped over my ears to mute the sound a little. On either side of me, the witch and the wise-woman sat calmly listening. The list of names seemed endless, many of them strange, foreign-sounding names in languages I did not know. And then suddenly, I heard: "Edward Johnson, Ted Henry, Colin Phillips . . ." These were the names of the men who had perished aboard the *Free Spirit* just last night. I heard Johnny's brother's name called last of all. Then the voice fell silent, and there was only the splash of the ocean waves and the whispering of the wind.

The significance of that silence finally dawned on my dazed mind. "He's alive," I whispered aloud, feeling a terrible weight fall from my heart. "He's alive."

I didn't realize I was crying until Jezebel—of all people—gruffly handed me a handkerchief to wipe my eyes. The wise-woman and the witch lifted my trembling body and guided me out of the ruin. On the beach I was blindfolded again and led down the twisty paths toward the cottage and home. All the dark, stumbling way, my heart sang over and over in my chest: "He's alive. He's alive."

Hannah released me from the blindfold and gave me a hug before sending me home to my bed. As I reached the edge of town, an owl flapped over my head and landed on a nearby fencepost. "We scryed for him again," the bird cried, speaking in Jezebel's voice. "The ship was in Manila for repairs after being damaged in a storm. They are on the way home now and should arrive in port a week from today if the weather stays fair."

The owl leapt into the air again before I could speak, and as it sailed away, I heard it call: "You were a brave girl. Well done."

A week to the day after hearing the voice in the watchtower, I was running down the dock toward a tall figure who dropped his bags and swept me into his arms. Johnny and I were married the next morning, and sitting side by side in the front pew of the church were the wise-woman and the witch, both of whom would one day act as godmothers to our numerous children.

15

The White Wizard

Looking at him, no one would ever guess that Edward Dimond was a wizard. He didn't look the part. Instead of flowing robes he wore breeches and a simple shirt. Instead of a long gray beard, he was clean-shaven. Instead of wild hair and a hooked nose, he had curly white hair and a Grecian profile. And instead of a high tower filled with bubbling beakers and skulls, he lived in a lovely cottage surrounded by flower gardens that abutted the town cemetery. Yet in spite of all this, Edward Dimond was indeed a wizard. And a cracking good one at that.

Now, you may be wondering why a known wizard was tolerated in this pious community, but the fact is that Edward Dimond was a white wizard. The minister believed him to be a prophet in the tradition of Moses, who made magical signs before the pharaoh of Egypt, and many of the people in the community thought he wasn't a man at all. When they spoke of "angels among us" or "a messenger of God," they were referring to Edward.

Folks said that Edward Dimond could influence the weather, see visions, predict the future, and look into the past. He had helped poor widows recover stolen goods, changed blackguards and thieves into honest men, and aided the sea captains on their voyages. Folks were frightened of his abilities, but he was still considered a valuable asset to most everyone in town.

Now, my family lived right down the lane from Edward, and I had known him all my life. We were sailors, the men in my family, and while Father was at sea, Edward kept an eye on our steadily growing family. I was the youngest boy of four, and in some respects Edward was closer to me than Da, who was sometimes away for years at a time.

When Da was home, he sternly instructed us to treat Master Dimond with respect, for the old man had saved the life of many a sailor, calling out to them through the howling winds and beating rain of a storm to direct their ships to safety. I was never quite sure what he meant when he said this, but it sounded most impressive.

One of my first memories was slipping into the graveyard to watch Edward working his magic spells. He was a weather wizard, and he could summon the thunder, clear the mist, calm all but the most raging storms, and bring rainbows out of a clear blue sky. I sat very still and watched Edward with his patched jacket and wild white hair passing among the tombstones. He walked in a broad circle and then bent and wrote something in the dirt. When he finished writing, the outer edge of the circle flared with sudden light and then went dark.

Safe inside this magic fortress, Edward picked up a pitcher of water lying at his feet and poured it on the top of a long, flat tomb. Instead of dribbling off the edges, the water began to swirl around, and it took on the appearance of the sea. The water turned a turquoise blue like the waters that Da had described in the Caribbean, and I saw many tropical islands dotting the area

THE WHITE WIZARD

between massive coral reefs. Toward the bottom of this watery map, a massive storm brewed, and Edward watched it carefully. He spoke a few words in a language I didn't recognize. The words made red sparks dance in front of my eyes and made my ears fizz for a moment. Then a yellow light appeared, heading directly into the storm. The yellow light gradually took the shape of a ship. Edward watched it, frowning, for a moment, then he passed his hand over it and started nudging it toward calmer water. Within a few minutes, the glowing yellow ship was safely out of the storm and heading toward harbor on one of the tropical islands.

"'Tis the *Sparrowhawk*, Silas," Edward said conversationally toward the tombstone where I was hiding as he dismantled the spell. "I could sense she was heading into danger, so I came here to see what I could do."

Tucking the pitcher under one arm, he caught me by the hand and swung me upright. Keeping hold of my small hand, he led me from the cemetery. "I watch over them," he continued. "All the ships that sail out of our harbor, and many others beside. I watch over your Da, too. You may tell your Mother to expect him home Thursday week with a fine cargo and many presents for all of you."

He patted my head then and sent me skipping home with the news that would bring a relieved smile to my Mother's face. Even so young, I knew that she worried all the time while Da was at sea.

Edward's wife died when I was eight, and Mother sort of adopted him after that. The old man attended all the family gatherings and was there on the dock when we waved Da and my oldest brother Thaddeus off to sea. It was Thaddeus's first voyage as cabin boy, and he was extremely proud.

It was Edward who came to us, gray-faced, a month later, with the news. A sudden storm near Jamaica had blasted Da's ship. Edward had stood spelling and shouting in the cemetery for hours, trying to save her. But she had gone down with all hands, and Thaddeus and my father were dead. Mother gave a gasp and then laughed bitterly. "I knew it," she whispered to herself. "I felt it in my bones." Her face was pale and grave, and her shoulders slumped forward—a slump they carried the rest of her life. That was the last time I remember hearing her laugh.

The next few months were a blur. Da had not left us much money, though we owned the house free and clear. Mother found apprenticeships for my two remaining brothers, but I was too young, so I stayed home with her and went to school and did the chores and earned money as an errand boy. Edward visited us every day and kept us informed about the whereabouts and well-being of each of my brothers when they grew old enough to become sailors themselves.

I went to sea when I was sixteen. Mother was resigned to my going. Three of her men were at sea now, but my sister-in-law Emma and her little girls lived with Mother while my brother Paul was at sea, so she was not alone. I took to sailing like a duck to water. Seafaring was in our blood from way back, and it was the life for me. Whenever we were becalmed or a storm blew up, I knew that the white wizard of Marblehead, my adopted grandfather Edward Dimond, was keeping an eye on me by his enchanted grave in the cemetery, and I felt safe.

One day in late autumn, my ship was off Block Island and heading home toward Marblehead when a granddaddy of a storm hit us head on. Waves as high as mountains smashed us from side to side. The ship went straight up one side—so steep I thought she'd fall over backward—and then straight down the other. Finally, battered, bruised, and half-dead, the ship and her crew outrode the storm. But before we could get our bearings, a horrible, thick fog descended. We couldn't see one another from a foot away, and the ship was still driven forward by the waves caused by that terrible storm. We hove to and tried to anchor, but the massive waves carried us forward until the storm anchor broke loose and set us adrift.

I was at the helm, wondering despairingly which way to go and what to do. We couldn't use the sextant to shoot the sun and figure our latitude until the fog lifted, and chances were we'd be aground on a reef and drowning in the depths before that happened. A wind sprang up, but it only made the fog boil and billow over the ship, doing nothing to lift it.

As the fog swirled around me, I cast a quick, desperate look at my compass. And was slapped in the head by a sudden sharp wind that felt like a schoolmaster disciplining an erring child.

"North by northwest, Silas. Now! Quick, man!" The voice of Edward Dimond rang out right above my head. In the same moment, another gust of wind slapped the back of my head for emphasis. I turned the wheel north by northwest.

"Now keep her steady as she goes, Silas," Edward's voice snapped above my head. My whole body was shaking with fear, for off to the east I could now hear breakers. Footsteps sounded through the fog as the captain came running to my side, having heard the voice of the Wizard of Marblehead.

"Wizard Dimond," he gasped.

"The Cape is dead ahead," Dimond's voice said from above

my head. "You almost hit the reef. West, Silas, on my mark. Now!"

I turned the ship sharply in the blind fog, trusting Edward to guide us through. For hours, and then days, we fought the waves and the wind and the fog, helmsmen, crew, and captain following orders from the voice that boomed above our heads. And then the fog lifted; the lookout sang out "Land ho"; and we found ourselves right off Marblehead and heading in to harbor.

Mother and Edward met us on the dock, and Mother snatched me to her heart, crying in an ecstasy of relief while the captain and the rest of the crew pounded Edward on the back and everyone tried to shake his hand at once. The little white-haired Wizard of Marblehead had saved our lives, and there were no words to express our gratitude. In my mind's eye, I could imagine him leaning over the water-topped tombstone for three days, guiding us tirelessly through the fog to our home port. And indeed, he looked weary beyond belief. I started to speak, then fell silent. But the smile we exchanged said all we had to say without words. I knew that he considered this success at least a partial repayment to me and Mother for his failure to save Da all those years ago.

And right there on the dock, for the first time since Da and Thaddeus died, we both heard my Mother laugh.

16

The Black Horse

Now Sam Hart, he was a rascal. A charming man, with a talent for gambling and a good eye for horses, but a rascal nonetheless. He was the despair of his old mother, whose deepest wish was to have her Sam settle down and raise a family. Every time a young lady's name was paired with Sam, old Mrs. Hart would cackle with glee, only to have her hopes crushed again.

Sam's keen eye for horseflesh and his amazing seat soon put him at the forefront of all the local races. After he bought a gorgeous bay mare with some of his gambling winnings, there was no stopping him. That mare could outrun every living creature for miles around—and not just horses, either! Sam called her Fire-eater, and he boasted about her up and down the county until folks would leave the general store or smithy to avoid listening to him.

It was agreed that everyone in town wanted Sam taken down a peg or two, but there truly was no one who could do it. Until the day a dark stranger came to town, riding a black horse. The dignified figure atop the horse was sober of clothing, with a closely shaven face, a simple cocked hat, and a white wig. In short, he looked like a visiting parson—until you looked into his wicked, deep-set black eyes and caught an occasional red gleam in their depths. The stranger rode right up to Sam's place, where the rascal was smoking a pipe on the front porch.

"I've got a horse here that is a match for that mare of yours, Sam Hart," the stranger said without preamble. "He is a true 'fire-eater,' and can beat your mare without breaking a sweat."

"Rubbish," Sam Hart snapped, taking an instant dislike to the boastful man with his gorgeous black horse. The horse gleamed in the rays of the afternoon sunlight, his muscles rippling softly just beneath his skin.

"Three-to-one," the stranger said at once, "with my horse thrown into the bargain if I lose."

By this time, several neighbors had gathered in the street to look at the beautiful black horse and listen in on the conversation.

"I won't bet my mare," Sam said sharply, glaring defiantly from the stranger to the crowd.

"I didn't ask you to," the stranger said smoothly, smiling at the crowd.

"What's the matter, Sam? Afraid he'll beat you?" called the tanner, who lived next door. Sam's eyes almost popped out of his head with rage when he heard his neighbor crowing with malicious delight.

At that moment, Sam's old mother hobbled through the door to see what was going on. Hearing the tanner's taunt, she said: "My Sammy doesn't take bets. He's a fine Christian boy who needs a wife."

She peered hopefully at young Elizabeth, the tanner's pretty, spirited daughter, who had grown up right next door and for whom Sam rarely had a kind word to say. Elizabeth gave Sam an impish grin and a mocking wave.

"I won't be courted by a coward," she said in a high, clear voice that reached every ear in the crowd. The neighbors roared their delighted agreement with this sentiment, eddying around the stranger and his black horse. The magnificent beast stood like a stone amid the ruckus. Not a muscle twitched. The stranger was equally silent, his eyes fixed on Sam Hart.

Like all boasters, Sam hated to be mocked, especially by Elizabeth, who was sharp and sweet and who would not give her rascally neighbor the time of day. Sam, who secretly admired his beautiful neighbor, was stung mightily by Elizabeth's declaration. Sam had long ago decided that if he ever did marry someone, that someone would be Elizabeth. Yet here she stood, scorning him as a coward. He turned bright red. "I accept your bet," he said to the stranger on the black horse.

"Oh, Sammy, such wild behavior," his old mother cried. "You'll never get a wife now. Oh, Elizabeth, I am sorry!" With a wail of grief, she tossed her apron over her head and rushed back into the house.

To the crowd, this performance was as good as comic theater. They laughed aloud and mocked Sam, who stomped off the porch and headed out to his barn to saddle the bay mare. By the time he returned, riding his swift Fire-eater, the course had been decided. The race was to begin at Central Square and end at Woburn Common, and the stranger even offered to give Sam and his mare a ten-rod head start. If the magnificent black horse caught the mare's tail in his teeth before they reached Woburn Common, the stranger won the bet. If not, then the money and the black horse belonged to Sam.

Sam flushed with rage when the stranger proposed giving him a head start—*a head start!*—but the crowd, which had grown exponentially by this time, was all for it. And Elizabeth's mocking grin dared him to complain aloud. He wanted to shake her until she stopped grinning. No, he wanted to kiss her until she stopped grinning and begged him to kiss her again. Sam pushed the thought out of his mind as he walked the mare to the starting line drawn up by the tanner.

Several townsmen and women were dispatched to the Common to draw a finish line, and Elizabeth was among them. Sam watched her go and then grimly turned his attention back to the silent stranger on the magnificent black horse. The horse was dancing a little now in anticipation, quivers running over his skin. He snorted and cocked an eye at Fire-eater, who snorted and cocked an eye in return. What a foal these two would have, Sam thought suddenly.

A few minutes later, the newsboy came trotting up on his pony to announce that the finish line was set and the race could begin. At once, the order was given, a whip cracked, and Sam and his mare sprang off on their "head start" to the cheers and boos of the crowd. Rapidly, too rapidly, the black horse followed them. It bridged the large gap as if it were nothing, and the black horse was not even panting as it drew ever closer to the withers of galloping Fire-eater.

Sam glanced back over his shoulders into a pair of glowing red eyes underneath the cocked hat, and he saw that the black horse was snorting fire from his nostrils and mouth. At that moment, Sam's racing heart nearly stopped. He knew that it was the Devil behind him, and that to lose this race was to forfeit more than money.

With his eternal soul on the line, Sam crouched over the neck of the sweating Fire-eater, urging her forward as fast as she could run. They were nearing the midpoint of the race, and suddenly he could hear Elizabeth's voice cheering him onward. He risked a glance to the side and saw her perched on top of a fence post, blue eyes gleaming with pride. He saw her glance back at the rival horse, who was moving forward at an unearthly pace, hooves sparking, fire burning from mouth and eyes. Then she looked at the tall dark stranger riding that maniacal horse. As she stared at him, the stranger's cocked hat blew off his head, revealing glowing red eyes and a small pair of horns on his head.

"Sam!" Elizabeth screamed aloud in horror. "Sam! It's the Devil!"

Sam tore his eyes away from his sweet young neighbor and concentrated on keeping the mare's tail away from the black horse. There had to be something he could do! There was always a way out. But how? Then he thought of it.

At the next corner, he turned Fire-eater away from the Common, heading toward the Baptist church. The black horse was at the mare's heels, his teeth snapping as he reached for her tail. Sam was headed for the church door, trying to reach holy ground, but was forced away by the black horse's snapping jaws and so raced his mare instead in a circuit around the church. Once, twice, they circled the churchyard, the Devil and his black horse hard on their heels. Fire-eater was tired now, and Sam knew without question that this was his last chance to circle the church. If they didn't reach holy ground this time, he would forfeit his soul.

The mare seemed to sense his thought, for she put on a sudden burst of speed, heading toward the church door. But the

THE BLACK HORSE

black horse was right behind them, and one more leap would put the mare's tail in his teeth. Sam gasped, hope fading from his heart, but the mare gave a sudden wild leap, burst through the church door, and skidded across the foyer. Behind her, the black horse pulled up short and whinnied, pouring forth a stream of fire from its open mouth that singed the mare's tail and Sam's flapping coat. Then it dropped to its knees while Sam turned the mare with difficulty in the small entryway of the church. He watched as the Devil dismounted.

"Sam Hart, you cheated," the Devil said grimly, but there was a grin plucking the corner of his mouth. "However, since you have just cheated the worst of all cheaters, I will own to being beaten."

As he spoke, Elizabeth came running and sobbing into the churchyard, her hair falling out of its decorous bun, and her eyes wild with fear. She stopped suddenly, staring at the kneeling black horse, the tall Devil beside it, and Sam atop his mare inside the foyer of the church.

"Here's your money," the Devil said, ignoring the panting, wide-eyed girl. "You'll need it for a wedding, I hear. But you'll have to catch the moneybag, for I cannot enter that benighted place you call a church." So saying, he flung a bag full of gold to Sam, who silently caught it with one hand. "And take my horse as well. He'll be as safe as your mare after I'm gone. His name is Lucifer."

With a wicked smile, the Devil bowed, first to Elizabeth and then to Sam. Then he vanished in a puff of sulfurous smoke that made them both cough and gasp. When the smoke cleared, they were alone in the churchyard.

"Well, Elizabeth," Sam said shakily. "Do I need this money for a wedding?"

She gasped, tears streaming suddenly from her eyes. "Y . . . yes, Sam," she said simply, moving forward to grasp the bridle of the black horse and urge him to his feet.

Carefully, Sam rode Fire-eater out of the church and over to his new fiancé, who had flung herself into the saddle of the black horse in a most unladylike way. Elizabeth was a champion racer herself, and she handled the black horse with ease as they headed toward the Common to tell the townsfolk what had happened.

"Just one thing, Sam," Elizabeth said, pausing the black horse just before the road.

"What is it, love?" asked Sam, riding forward to take her hand. And it says a great deal about the force of his regard for

Elizabeth that at that moment he found it much more desirable to look deeply into her blue eyes than to gaze possessively at his magnificent new horse.

"I don't think we should call this horse Lucifer," Elizabeth said firmly. "I think we should call him Gabriel."

And that's exactly what they did. The black horse Gabriel went on to win every race in the county for many years, bringing fame and fortune to his owners. And the foals sired by Gabriel and Fire-eater were much prized through all of New England, and each of them was a champion racer.

17

Black Magic

SPRINGFIELD

He was a strange man; wild-eyed and hook-nosed, with a shock of black curls streaked with gray and the loping walk and crazy laugh of the insane. Folks in town avoided Mad Henry, who engaged in no visible profession yet somehow always had money. He lived in a large, decrepit mansion, from which strange lights shone at night. Folks said he was a black magician who called upon the powers of darkness to wreck havoc upon his neighbors. Others claimed he was a mad doctor trying to restore life to foul corpses he dug up from the local cemetery. Rumors spread across the whole region regarding Mad Henry, but no one ever dared ask him what it was he did in his lonely mansion at night.

Young boys looking for a thrill looked no further than the windows of that benighted dwelling. Strange and grotesque shapes could be seen through the curtains when the moon was full, and many a tough lad went running from the place, weeping with fright. Most of them spent the next month plagued by the nightmarish memories of what they had seen.

Now it happened one year that a new attorney opened an office in town, bringing with him his young family. The eldest daughter, Rachel, was a beauty and soon became the belle of local society. Mad Henry saw her through his bedroom window one night as she strolled arm-in-arm with two of her girlfriends, and he fell in love with the red-haired minx at once with all the passion in his twisted soul. The very next evening, he showed up on her doorstep carrying a bunch of red roses that gleamed with their own inner light and left dewdrops of pure gold on the maiden's mantelpiece long after their giver made his way home.

Rachel was both intrigued and frightened by her strange suitor, who was so very much older than she. Her father was pleased by her new beau. Yes, Mad Henry was a strange fellow, but he was obviously well-off and could keep his daughter in the style she deserved. And he showered the lovely red-haired maiden with gifts—goblets of pure gold, necklaces of pearl and diamond, and stranger things too. Like the statue of a small dog that could actually bark and wag its tail; a mirror that reflected far-off vistas when it was not being used by its owner; and a pot of daisies—Rachel's favorite flower—that never grew old nor dropped a single petal, even if it was not watered for a week.

The gifts made Rachel uneasy. She couldn't help wondering what price their owner had paid to create them. Folks in town whispered that Mad Henry had sold his soul to the Devil in exchange for the ability to turn lead into gold. Alchemist, they called him, and other, darker names. He never invited Rachel or her parents into his home. He never brought anyone there, and Rachel was afraid to ask why.

About this time, young Geoffrey Simmons, the son of a prominent businessman in town, came home from university, where he was studying to be a doctor. He met Rachel at a party given in his honor and fell head-over-heels for the attorney's daughter. Rachel found his simple love much easier to accept than the complex adoration offered to her by the alchemist. A week after they met, Geoffrey and Rachel eloped, leaving behind a bewildered and angry father and a stunned alchemist.

The elopement was a nine-day wonder in town. By the time Geoffrey and Rachel returned from their honeymoon, their marriage was an accepted fact, and though they were teased about its suddenness, everyone was happy for them. Rachel's parents threw a big ball for the newlyweds and invited everyone in town. It was a festive, happy occasion with music and dancing and special performers brought to town for the festivities.

Rachel had been acting jittery all evening, looking over her shoulder again and again, sitting out the dances, and laughing with a too-high pitch that suggested the red-haired bride was not really happy at all. Geoffrey noticed and pulled her into a small alcove to kiss and comfort her.

"Are you worried about Henry?" Geoffrey asked.

Rachel turned her head and nodded in agreement.

"Henry won't come," Geoffrey said. "He's a gentleman and will leave you alone."

"You don't know him," Rachel told her new husband. "He is not quite sane, Geoffrey. He will come for me."

"Nonsense!" Geoffrey scoffed gently. He gave her another kiss and then the couple returned to the dance.

Rachel was waltzing with her father when she heard the first clap of thunder. It boomed in the distance and gradually got louder until it became a continuous roar in the sky above the dance hall. Lightning flashed again and again, sizzling the air, but no rain fell. It was not that kind of storm.

The guests murmured in fear as the sound of the storm grew louder than the orchestra, and the music twanged and limped to a halt when lightning struck a tree directly outside the hall. Suddenly, the double doors blew open and a sharp, nasty breeze whirled in, bringing with it the smell of dead, decaying things and just a whiff of acrid chemicals. And then Mad Henry loomed in the doorway, black cape flapping in the foul breeze, pupils gleaming red with anger, wild black curls streaked with gray standing on end. He raised his arms above his head and shouted aloud in a language that made the eyes burn and the skin shiver.

There came a sharp clanking sound, and the grotesque figures of the dead came marching two by two into the room, decaying skeletons with bits of skin and dirt still clinging to them. Their eye sockets glowed with blue fire as they surrounded the room. Guests screamed aloud in terror and raced to escape out of every door and window. The boldest tried to attack the invaders, but those who tried found themselves pinned against the walls by hands of stretched gray skin and white bone.

Two of the creatures captured Geoffrey and threw him down at the feet of their lord amidst a shower of dirt and bits of gray skin that flaked from their foul forms. Geoffrey's head banged against the stone floor with a crack that left him stunned and helpless before the alchemist. Mad Henry stared at his rival with a gentle smile that boded ill for the university student. "Kill him," he ordered. "And bring me his widow."

Rachel screamed then, a terrible sound that made even the wild skeletons flinch. She ran forward, pushing through the confining ring of the dead, and flung herself upon her trembling young husband.

BLACK MAGIC

"Kill us both," she cried desperately, holding her husband close. "I will not go with you."

Mad Henry smiled grimly and nodded to his dead servants. They plucked the red-haired lass from her husband as if she weighed no more than a small child and marched her out the door. Her father leapt at the cadavers, beating at them with his walking stick; and one struck out with a decaying fist, catching the attorney a blow that broke his nose and sent shards of bone directly into his brain, killing him instantly. They carried the screaming, beating, writhing Rachel out into the thundering night, and none could stay their progress or pull the girl from their grisly hands.

Red eyes gleaming with evil satisfaction, Mad Henry drew a silver-bladed knife and casually cut the bridegroom's throat from ear to ear. The he whirled around, cape swirling about him like a black cloud, and strode from the room. Behind him, the army of the dead tossed their battered victims to the floor and followed their master, striding right through the large pool of blood that poured from the dying Geoffrey as he gasped out the final moments of his life. Behind them, the monsters left a trail of blood-stained footprints, half human and half skeleton, that burned themselves permanently into the stone floor of the dance hall.

Geoffrey's parents rushed to his side, and his mother pressed a handkerchief to the gaping wound on his throat in an ineffectual attempt to stop the bleeding. He gazed up at them with glazing eyes and gasped: "Find Rachel." And then he was gone.

The sounds of thunder and lightning were fading away as the alchemist and his dead companions disappeared into the dark night. Geoffrey's father patted his wife clumsily on the shoulder, went home for his gun, and then stalked through the streets of the town, heading toward the house of the local minister, who had stayed home from the party that night with a headache. Geoffrey's father didn't care if the man were dropping dead from consumption. He was determined to rouse the holy man at once and rescue his daughter-in-law.

As Geoffrey's father marched across town, he was joined by Rachel's two brothers, a cousin, and the fathers of her friends. The small mob pounded on the door of the minister's house, waking him and his wife and demanding he come with them at once to the home of the alchemist. They did not even give the poor preacher time to dress, dragging him along with them in nightshirt and cap, his glasses on upside-down and a Bible clutched in his hands.

When they arrived at the alchemist's house, they found it lit from top to bottom, and the stench of chemicals set all the men to gasping for breath and sneezing. Geoffrey's father seemed oblivious to the smell. He leapt into the house with his rifle, shouting aloud for Mad Henry to come down. Inspired by his courage, the mob spread out through the well-lit house, searching for the alchemist and his prisoner. They found nothing. Nothing at all. No furniture, no laboratory, not even dust and cobwebs. The house was completely empty save for the light, which shone from a series of mysterious globes that bobbed near the ceiling of each room. The alchemist had vanished.

The maddened mob torched the empty house and dragged the minister for miles through the surrounding woods and farms and fields, searching for Mad Henry and his prisoner, but they were gone. Search parties scoured the countryside for days, but turned up nothing. Geoffrey and Rachel's father were buried in the local cemetery, and the dance hall, whose stone floor was scored with the footprints of the dead, was torn down. No one in town spoke about what had happened, and no one dared imagine what had become of poor Rachel.

A year to the day after the ball, a timid knock sounded upon the door of Geoffrey's parents' home. When the father opened it, he saw a gaunt, gray figure on the stoop. Her eyes were dull with exhaustion and pain; her once-red hair was pure white and writhed wildly about her head. It took him a moment to realize that it was Rachel, but his wife knew at once and pulled the wretched figure into the house with exclamations of horror and pity. Rachel couldn't speak. Her tongue had been cut out. But she produced a knife from her tattered garments—the knife with a silver blade that they had last seen in the hands of the alchemist—and the gleam of satisfaction in Rachel's eyes told them that the streaks of blood that coated the knife were those of Mad Henry. Then Rachel fell into a dead faint. Geoffrey's parents carried her to Geoffrey's old room and summoned a doctor and her mother. But it was too late. Rachel died in her sleep that night, and upon her ravaged face was a smile of peace.

Inside her tattered dress, they found a note to her mother. It read:

Dearest Mother:

After many months of imprisonment and terrible suffering at the hands of the alchemist, I dug myself out of the stone tower where he kept me, clawing my way through loose mortar and stone until I was free. After his last gruesome visit to my cell, I followed the alchemist to his home deep in the dark woods near the tower. Mad Henry had taken my husband and my youth, and I was determined to take his life. And so I have, using the knife he used to kill my Geoffrey. If this condemns me in the eyes of God, so be it. I will die a murderess, and proud to be. Geoffrey and my father have been avenged, and I leave it to God to judge if I have done right or wrong.

Yours,
Rachel

18

Bean-Nighe

WORCESTER

I hurried through the grass and down the slope toward the stream, as the afternoon sun made the shadows dance around me and the wind soughed through the tall oak trees with a mournful sigh. My shoes crunched across the gravel drive and then took the steep trail that led to my favorite retreat. The path wound through the copse of trees where the stream meandered and bubbled. I could hear the rushing of the water as I climbed over a fallen birch tree. As my feet hit the large rock on the other side, I glanced down toward the rushing stream and smiled. The sound of flowing water always relaxed me. And I needed to relax. Things were not going well at home.

I climbed down the last few feet and perched on a giant rock at water's edge. Pulling my knees up to my chest for comfort, I wrapped my arms around them. Then I unwrapped one arm long enough to wriggle a peppermint stick out of the pocket of my skirt. Popping the end in my mouth, I gazed down at the sunlight dappling the water through the branches and leaves of the thick trees overhead. Tiny little fish were darting to and fro in the large, calm pool to the left of the rock. To the right of my perch, the stream grew shallow, and the water tripped happily over small stones.

In my mind, I was not seeing the stream. I was seeing Papa's face when the grim midwife told him to ride for the doctor. I was hearing the horse's hooves pounding the gravel as he rode down the drive. I was seeing Annie—the escaped slave-girl whom we were assisting on her way to Canada—taking my little brother Timothy by the hand and walking with him down the lane to stay with our neighbors while Mama had her baby. And my ears still rang with Mama's agonized screaming, which had driven me out of the house and down to this quiet spot.

I didn't want to think about Mama and the new baby we were all so eager to see.

So I thought about Annie, and how she had come to our house—which was one of the northern stations on the Underground Railroad—hungry and tired and weary from months of hiding and walking north. She'd seen the signal we'd set out on our gate and had come to the door for food and shelter.

Mama had welcomed her with open arms, and Annie, even in her exhausted state, had seen what my brother and I were too little to see: that Mama was very ill with this last pregnancy and should not be on her feet. By the time Papa got home that night, Mama was resting on the settee and Annie and I were baking cookies in the kitchen while my little brother supervised and did the taste-testing.

Papa was so relieved to see Mama at rest. The doctor was worried about her, but we were too poor to hire help—aside from a village girl who came once a week to help Mama with heavy work like laundry and cleaning. Papa rode out at once

BEAN-NIGHE

to make discreet enquiries to see if Annie were being seriously pursued by the authorities. To his relief, he found no signs or rumors of pursuit. Upon hearing this, Annie herself decided it was safe to stay with us and help Mama for a few weeks until the baby was born, in exchange for rest and shelter and a safe passage to Canada. Papa told everyone in town that Annie had come from Boston to work for us. Folks accepted the story without question and welcomed Annie into our tight-knit abolitionist community as Mother's helper and friend.

I don't know how long I sat there, watching the shadows grow longer and listening to the stream murmuring to itself. I didn't turn my head when I heard soft footsteps coming down the path, and I kept my eyes firmly on the moving water when Annie slipped onto the stone beside me.

"Your Papa is looking for you," she said. I thrust my lip forward to keep it from trembling. "He wants to talk to you."

"I already know," I said, dropping my head onto my arms to hide my trembling mouth. "The doctor didn't get here in time, did he?"

"No, Carrie, he didn't," Annie said softly, touching my black curls with a tender hand. "I'm so sorry. Your Mama is in Heaven now with your new baby brother."

She took me in her arms then and let me cry for my poor dead Mama and the tiny little baby brother I would never know. Then she took my hand, and we went up to the house, where my blue-eyed Papa was acting dazed and lost. Little Timothy had been left at the neighbor's house while arrangements were made for the wake and funeral.

The next two days were a blur to me. People kept coming to the house to weep and wail and hold us "poor, motherless

children." Papa's eyes had lost their twinkle, and he kept twisting his fingers in his curly dark beard and tugging on it until it must have hurt. Timothy wept all the time and kept calling for Mama. He thought she had gone to the village and would be back any moment. It was awful, and the worst part was the emptiness in that house full of people—an emptiness that could only be filled by one person—and she was gone.

Annie was a tower of strength in the midst of our pain. She and my grandmother prepared the food, helped Papa with the funeral arrangements, and washed and dressed my poor Mama's body. She and my tiny brother were laid in an open casket in the sitting room, and all our friends and neighbors came and wept over her. Since I was only eight and couldn't help much with the wake, I was put in charge of Timothy and did everything I could to distract him. He kept running into the sitting room and trying to climb into the casket with Mama, so Papa sent us outside to play. As if I could play. There was such a weight on my chest that I could barely breathe, and I wanted to cry, but I couldn't push the tears past the knot in my throat.

The next morning, the casket was placed in our carriage and driven first to the church and then to the graveyard next door. Timothy and I stood with Papa and Annie and my grandparents while the minister talked about Heaven—how beautiful it was and how happy Mama would be in that lovely place. I was fine until the moment they lowered the casket into the ground. That's when I finally realized that Mama wasn't coming back ever again. I screamed and tried to grab the ropes and pull her back up. Papa quickly caught me up in his arms and carried me away, sobbing my heart out.

When we got home, the house filled once again with visitors. Grandma and Annie went into action at once, rushing into the kitchen to put out food and accepting gifts of flowers and desserts and toys for me and Timothy. Papa wasn't quite able to cope with it all, and Grandma sent him to take a walk by the stream until he regained his composure. A few minutes later, Papa came bursting through the back door, his blue eyes wild with some emotion I didn't understand. He called to my Grandfather to come with him, and Grandfather went without question. Annie and Grandma were puzzled but didn't say anything. I don't think they wanted to frighten Timothy and me.

Papa and Grandfather came back about a half hour later. Papa slipped into the sitting room almost immediately to greet the gathered friends and neighbors, but Grandfather stopped in the kitchen to talk to Grandma and Annie. They spoke in low tones, and I couldn't hear what they were saying. Whatever it was made wrinkles of pain and worry crease Grandma's face, and Annie's happy mouth became a grim line.

After the guests had left, and Grandma and Grandpa departed, taking my little brother to spend the night at their place, Papa took me aside and told me that I was no longer allowed to play down by the stream. When I protested, he said: "I'm sorry, little love, but I forbid it. You will listen to me in this matter."

And that was that. I stormed and cried and protested, but he just gave a weary sigh, covered his eyes with a trembling hand, and asked Annie to put me to bed. This final statement took my breath away. Every night for my whole life, Papa had tucked me into bed and kissed me goodnight. And now, tonight of all nights, when my poor Mama lay under the ground with my

dead brother, he was abandoning his lifelong task. I broke into sobs and wailed on Annie's shoulder as she carried me upstairs, put me into my nightgown, and tucked me into bed.

It was summer and still light outside. I lay for a while looking at the ceiling and fuming about how unfair Papa was. Then I did something that was unusual for an obedient child like me. Heartsick and over-tired, I slipped out of my bed, threw on a dressing gown and slippers, and went down the back staircase and out into the yard. I didn't know why they wanted me to stay away from my favorite play-spot, and at that moment I didn't care. God had already taken my Mama from me, *and* the new baby that we had all wanted so badly. To also deprive me of my special retreat was the height of cruelty to my eight-year-old mind.

I marched through the grass and down the slope toward the stream as the setting sun deepened the shadows around me and the wind whistled through the tall oak trees with a mournful sound almost like that of the weeping and wailing I'd heard all afternoon at the house. I wanted to weep and wail myself, for I missed my Mama so badly. "Come back, Mama," I whispered aloud as my slippers crunched across the gravel path and I took the steep, winding trail that led to my favorite retreat.

The trail was dark and eerie. Dusk had already fallen among the copse of trees where the stream meandered and bubbled. I could hear the rushing of the water as I climbed over the fallen birch tree. As my feet hit the large rock on the other side, I peered through the gloom toward the rushing stream. And I saw her. My Mama. She was kneeling at the edge of the water with a tiny baby shirt in her hand. She was scrubbing at it with a brush, washing it clean. I had seen her scrubbing our clothes thus a hundred times or more, but never by the stream. Always at the house, in the big washtub, with the help of the neighbor girl Papa had hired to assist my poor overworked Mama with the chores once a week.

"Mama!" I shouted, breaking into a run at the sight of her. My heart pounded with joy and relief. They'd gotten it wrong: Papa, the doctor, Annie, the minister. Mama wasn't dead. She was right here.

Mama turned her head at the sound of my voice and I froze in my tracks, one foot still lifted. Her eyes glowed blue-green in their sockets, and her nose had only one nostril. Her face and hands were gray and hollow, with dark veins popping out here and there. She looked as if she'd been dead for a long time, not just two days. One tooth was visible through her withered lips, and her torso was as twisted and dried as her lips. The baby shirt she held in one hand was full of blood, as was the brush she held in the other. And the water of the merry, bubbling stream was swirling red with blood too. My horrified gaze went to the basket of baby clothes beside her, laying damp and stained in an ever-expanding pool of blood.

I couldn't move. I couldn't scream or wail or hide my eyes. I just stood there and stared at the hideous, warped representation of my beloved Mama and wanted to be sick. But I couldn't even throw up. Our eyes remained locked together for a long moment. Then Mama lifted the hand holding the scrub brush and beckoned to me. My heart pounded so hard it hurt my ribs, but I had to go to her. I had to. This was my mother.

Then I heard a voice.

"Oh, no, Miz O'Toole. You already have one child with you. You don't need another." It was the clear voice of Annie, speaking from somewhere behind me. I felt the slave-girl's arms fling themselves around my small body, and she swung me up as if I weighed nothing at all. Her touch broke the spell I was under. I gasped desperately once, twice, and then threw up all over poor Annie. She bore it stoically, and held me—sick and tired and covered with the disgusting remains of my dinner—as I sobbed and sobbed my heart out in her arms. Somehow, I knew that my Mama was no longer washing clothes by the stream, though I didn't turn and look as Annie carried me back to the house.

"We told you not to go down there, Carrie," Annie said, scolding me gently as she cleaned me up and tucked me back into bed. "But I knew you would. Stubborn, that's what you are." She wiped away a few more tears from my cheeks.

"I don't understand," I wailed suddenly, all the pent-up emotion coming out in a high-pitched sob. "You said Mama went to Heaven. But she's down by the creek and she's . . . she's . . . " I couldn't go on.

At that moment, the door to my room burst open and Papa came in, dark hair disheveled, blue eyes sad over his curly dark beard. He nodded to Annie, who left the room quietly, and then he knelt beside my bed and took me into his huge arms. I broke into sobs again, and Papa cried with me. When we had both calmed a little, I whispered: "I don't understand, Papa. Why isn't Mama in Heaven?"

"Oh, my little love, I would have spared you this," Papa groaned into my black curls. "It happens this way sometimes, when an Irishwoman dies in childbirth near a stream. Sometimes her ghost returns as a *bean-nighe*—a little washer by the stream. Some strange compulsion forces the ghost to wash and wash the clothes of the child she lost, as if erasing the blood will erase the event and bring the child back to life. According to your Grandfather, the *bean-nighe* will continue washing the clothes—both those of her dead child and of all who die in this place—for the rest of the days she would have lived if childbirth had not claimed her before her time. Only when she reaches the day that she would have died of natural causes is she released to Heaven."

I gave a great gasp of relief when I heard that Mama would some day go to Heaven. I was so afraid that I would never see her again—the real her, I mean, not the strange creature with her face that now washed in vain down by the stream.

"We will be leaving this place, Carrie," Papa continued after a long pause. "It is not fair to you or Timothy or me to stay here where we can see the *bean-nighe* by the creek. Your grandmother will take us in for the present, until I can sell the house and find a new place to live."

I nodded my head and lay my head against his chest uncertainly. I did not want to see the creature with Mama's face again, and yet it hurt me deep inside to leave it all alone by the creek.

"Can Annie come with us?" I asked finally in a tiny voice, rubbing my wet cheeks with the back of my hand.

"Annie is coming with us," Papa said at once, and I thought I heard a smile in his voice. "She will help take care of you at Grandma's house. And next week, you and Timothy and I will drive her up to Canada, where she can be a free woman at last."

I lifted my head and gave him a watery smile.

"That would make Mama glad," I said. He choked a bit and nodded.

"Yes, it would," he replied. Then he kissed me and tucked me into bed.

I waited until he left to tiptoe to the window and peer down toward the stream. The yard and woods were dark now, and I could see nothing save the light from the kitchen window below me. But in my mind, I saw the *bean-nighe* down at the stream, washing and washing, for all the years of her normal lifespan.

At that moment, I decided that I wouldn't think of the *bean-nighe* as Mama. My Mama was dead and gone. If something was compelling her spirit to linger here at the stream, it would not hold her forever, and I would see her again someday. That thought brought me some peace, and so I turned away from the window and climbed into bed, able to sleep at last.

19

The Brick Wall

CASTLE ISLAND, BOSTON HARBOR

There is something very satisfying in the moment when I thrust the tip of my sword into the lying, cheating soldier's heart and watch him fall to the sandy ground outside the walls of Fort Independence, where I currently hold the post of captain. It is a clean blow that will take his life in a few hours. (I am nothing if not an expert swordsman.) Lieutenant Massey writhes a bit at my feet in the chill air of Christmas morning, just before losing consciousness. A job well done, I decide with a little nod, as I turn away from the dying man. The world will be a cleaner place without Robert Massey in it.

As the seconds cluster around the lieutenant, I clean my sword and sheath it. Then I walk away without looking back. Why should I soil my eyes further with the likes of Massey, a man who squeaked by on his charm and then cheated honest soldiers at cards? Good riddance to bad rubbish.

I enjoy the rest of the Christmas season on the base, in spite of the enmity displayed to me by the more common soldiers after Robert Massey dies. They had obviously been fooled by his charm. But not I. I can see through charm to the heart of a man. I pride myself on my ability and feel it is my duty to rid the world of the cheats and liars who worm their way into the military. I have dueled to the death with six other specimens as nasty as this one in the past and anticipate that I will do so again in the future, the world being as corrupt as it is.

The men under my command seem depressed in the weeks following the holiday, and I work them hard. They mention Massey frequently, and to my disgust a monument to the lying lieutenant is commissioned, to be erected upon the spot where he died. I complain but am overruled by my pig-headed superiors.

I retreat to my chambers to sulk and soon am joined by a delegation of my men. Friends of Massey, all, I think they have come to complain about the duel we fought. I am surprised and delighted to learn, instead, that they have come to their senses and now see the lieutenant for the liar and cheat he really was. We share a round of drinks and laugh together over their mistake. One drink leads to another until even I, who am famed for my tolerance of strong alcohol, am feeling rather tipsy.

The other soldiers are worse off than I, of course, and someone suggests as a lark that we explore the lower dungeons. An odd fancy, that, but one that I find alluring after consuming a few more drinks. Everyone sets off in merry spirits, drinking and singing and laughing, our voices echoing through the narrow passages. Deeper and deeper we go, and I suggest we search for phantoms along the way. The men cheer and begin making spooky noises that seem appropriate to the dark and dusty paths we are traveling.

In spite of my good head for spirits, my head is spinning and my legs feel like rubber. I sag a little, and one of the good ol' chaps supports me. I am surprised to see that it is Massey's best friend, but am in too happy a mood to wonder for long. He smiles as we stagger along and sings the words of a bawdy song with me. Another of Massey's cronies grabs my other arm when I trip, and the three of us chant together to the amusement of the other men.

Things go a bit dim for me at this point. I am afraid I might even have passed out from too much drink—how embarrassing. When I come to, I am lying on my back in one of the dim old dungeons. After a moment, I realize that my wrists and ankles are shackled to the floor. Obviously another lark of some kind, I think, yanking against my restraints.

"Very funny, lads," I call out, turning my head toward the sound of voices and activity at the entrance to the cell. "Now set me free."

The soldiers don't answer me. A moment passes, then two. Then Massey's best friend appears holding mortar and a mason's trowel, and the other men begin handing him bricks. I realize that the soldiers are bricking up the entrance to the cell in which I lay shackled. "Very funny," I say again, louder this time. "Are you trying to teach me a lesson, lads? Is that what this trick is about? Make me sorry that I fought the duel with Massey? Because I'm not."

No one answers me. They work in silence, laying brick after brick until one row is done, then two. They are playing a game with me, of course. It is only a joke, I think. But something in the men's silence, in the way they build the wall more and more quickly, in the way they watch me with eyes that gleam in the dim light of the lantern makes the hair stand up on my head and brings shivers to my body. If this is a joke, it is a nasty one.

THE BRICK WALL

Massey's best friend pauses in his work and looks directly into my eyes. At that moment I realize that this joke is no joke. The soldiers mean to bury me alive in this dungeon. I scream then, tugging hard at the shackles that bind me. Scream after scream rips from my throat as I struggle against my bonds. I hope that my screams will be heard by others who will come and rescue me. But this dungeon is too deep within the fort, I fear. No one will hear. No one will come. I will be entombed alive and written off the books as a deserter.

They are on the final row of bricks. I am reduced to bribery now, but no one speaks. No one heeds me. As the last few bricks are mortared into place, I begin to cry like a pitiful baby and beg the men to spare me this terrible fate. No one answers.

I watch in heart-thudding horror as the last brick is put in place, as the last chink of light fades from my sight. Then I am in utter darkness. I howl in panic, writhing against the iron manacles binding hands and feet and twisting my body this way and that in a frenzy, trying to get free before it is too late—although somewhere in my mind, I know that it is already too late. Eventually I fall back against the floor, spent by my thrashings. My wrists and ankles are wet with my own blood, and the pain of the split skin is an agony almost as deep as that within my mind.

My fingers are torn and throbbing from their intense scrabbling against the hard floor. My mind rails against the darkness, against the utter heartlessness that has trapped me here alive. I find myself weeping angrily, though I have never shed a tear in my lifetime. My lifetime, which can now be counted in hours. Hours! "Oh, God, save me," I whimper. But if my fellow soldiers have not offered me mercy, then how can God?

The agony of the thought sends me writhing again in spite of the horrible pain racking my wrists, ankles, and hands. Daylight. I must see daylight again. One more time. Just once more.

"Don't leave me here to die alone! Don't leave me!"

My voice echoes again and again in my ears, growing fainter as within me a terrible thirst grows. Water. I crave water, but there is no one to give me a drink. No one.

I am alone, and the sheer brutal horror of it overwhelms me more than the terrible thirst growing in my mouth and throat, and the throbbing pain of my self-inflicted injuries. My eyes strain against the complete and utter darkness, and I wonder if they are even open. The world inside my mind has dimmed, and it is only at greater and greater intervals that sheer terror arouses me from my stupor and makes me writhe in agony against the chains.

Dear God, I can't get out. *I can't get out. I CAN'T GET OUT!*

20

Thar She Blows!

NANTUCKET

The rope of the harpoon was tangled around his leg. He noticed it seconds after launching the weapon into the side of the sperm whale they were tracking. With a gasp of panic, he reached for his knife. He had to free himself immediately. The rope was already tightening under the frantic movements of the whale. But his knife was not in its sheath.

The rope was biting deeply into his leg, and the pain was excruciating. He tugged at it with wet, salty fingers that were numb with cold. Then the whale dove and he plunged toward the edge of the boat. He heard his shipmates yell in alarm, felt them grabbing for him, and then he was over the side and plunging down, down into the depths of the sea, following the dying whale.

He thrashed about, still trying to free himself, and made the mistake of gasping when the rope sliced his leg half-off. The gasp drew water deep into his lungs and he choked and coughed, trying not to breathe as his chest seared with pain and spots appeared before his eyes.

The captain woke with a gasp of terror and reflexively started coughing, trying to expel from his lungs the burning water that existed only in his dreams. His wife rolled over in alarm as he wheezed and hacked, his leg still throbbing in pain from the cut of the rope.

"Darling, are you well?" she whispered, trying to minister to him without waking the baby.

"F . . . fine," he managed after a moment, taking in several breathes to steady himself.

In the cradle suspended from the cabin ceiling by four chains, the baby gave a couple of whimpers and then went back to sleep. The captain relaxed at the familiar sound and stared at the dark bulk of the cradle in the dim light. Rock-a-bye baby, he thought, and the simple words soothed him.

"It was only a dream," he said, as much to ease his own mind as that of his worried wife. He lay back among the covers and pulled her close to comfort them both. "Only a dream."

He ignored his still-burning lungs and the soft throb of pain in his leg. It was harder to ignore the fear of death that made his heart hammer in his chest. And the supernatural dread that accompanied it. The dream was so real . . . like a warning. Was he going to die tomorrow? The thought made him shudder, and he scolded himself for taking such a dismal view of things. It was just a dream, he told himself firmly, snuggling closer to his sleeping wife. Her warmth comforted him as nothing else could have done, and he felt himself relax. Perhaps it was not the common thing for the captain of a whaling vessel to bring his family along on the long journey, he mused, but in moments such as this, he rejoiced in his decision. His tension slowly eased, and he went back to sleep.

They were one year into their whaling run and had already bagged several of the monsters of the deep, though not a coveted sperm whale. Still, the captain considered their haul to be a profitable one, with three more years to go before they headed home to Nantucket. He was working on the log book the next morning when he heard the lookout shout: "Thar she blows!"

It brought everyone on board up to the deck at a dead run, in time to see a mighty sperm whale breaching off the weather beam.

"Lower the boat, boys," he shouted to his mates.

"We'll get 'im, captain," called wiry Nat Taylor, the harpooner under the second mate. He was a bold seaman with an eye patch and a rascally grin, and he laughed in delight as the men scrambled for the boats.

"Remember your knives," the captain shouted after them, suddenly recalling his nightmare. He wasn't sure if the men heard him.

According to the lookout, the sperm whale was still cruising on the surface. If they were lucky, it would stay up until the boats were in range. The captain prayed for good luck as he watched the boats—each with a six-man crew—chasing after it. So far, so good. He saw Nat ready the harpoon as the first boat approached the whale. Nat darted it, and then quickly readied and darted the second harpoon. And that's when it happened. The bowline somehow got wrapped around Nat's leg, and no one spotted it until the whale ran, dragging Nat overboard with him. The men grabbed for the harpooner, but he slipped through their hands, and in their panic the lurching sailors capsized the boat.

One boat stripped off the chase to rescue the capsized crew, while a second raced after the whale, determined to rescue Nat if they could. The whale dove—deep, deep, taking the lines and Nat with it. They never saw the whale or the harpooner again.

The crew was solemn and sad that night, and for many nights to come. Nat was the best harpooner they had on board and was well-liked by all. The captain had a service for him the night of the aborted whale-hunt, and his wife sang a beautiful hymn that choked up even the most hard-bitten of the sailors.

The next month passed with nary a whale sighting, and the captain began to wonder if the death of Nat had jinxed the ship. He started spending more time on deck with his telescope, straining his eyes again and again in the hope that he might spot something his eagle-eyed lookout had not.

He was standing alone at the railing one fine afternoon in early May when he felt the temperature around him plummet. He shivered and glanced up. Above his head, floating up by the rigging, was the glowing blue-white figure of a drowned man wearing an eye patch. It was the ghost of Nat Taylor. The captain gasped and shuddered at the sight. Wordlessly, the phantom lifted its hand and pointed off the starboard bow. Then it vanished, and as it did, he heard the lookout calling: "Thar she blows!"

There came the thunder of feet as the men ran from everywhere on the ship to launch the whaleboats. It was a right whale this time, and the capture went without a hitch. Two harpoons in, a short run by the whale, and then the crew pulled the boat up to the whale to make the kill.

"Chimney's afire" the captain told his wife when he saw the whale make its final blood-red spout. "We've got it now!"

The whale was secured to the boat, towed tail first back to

THAR SHE BLOWS!

the ship, and tied alongside the starboard side. Most of the crew spent the next several days harvesting the whale.

The men sang sea shanties as they worked cheerfully over the dead whale. It was good to be busy again. The captain watched them thoughtfully, but he told no one about seeing the ghost of the dead harpooner just before the whale appeared. He wasn't sure why Nat had come to him, and he didn't want anyone on the crew thinking there was a ghost aboard. It would make the men nervous, and they might get to thinking that the journey was jinxed.

Several times over the next two years, the figure of the drowned harpooner appeared to the captain just prior to the sighting of another whale. No one else seemed to see it, and the captain never spoke of it to anyone.

They were almost home to Nantucket the last time the captain saw Nat Taylor's ghost. The harpooner appeared suddenly, sitting on the rail next to the captain. This time, Nat appeared as he had in life, with his rascally grin and a glint in his unpatched eye.

"You've had a profitable run, captain," he said cheerfully.

"We have," the captain agreed quietly, lest the men hear him talking aloud to himself and think their captain had gone mad. "Although I'd rather we'd had a poor run and kept you with us, Nat."

"T'weren't meant to be, captain," Nat said sadly. "Anyway, I've done me best to send you some good fat whales. I want you to make sure my missus gets my share of the takings to help tide her over the rough patch. That's why I come back to help."

"We'll take care of her, Nat," the captain promised. "You have my word on it."

"Good." The ghost nodded awkwardly several times. Then his glowing face lit up with his rascal's grin. "Here's one more whale to remember me by! Don't forget your promise!"

As Nat Taylor vanished, the lookout shouted: "Thar she blows!"

Looking across the waves, the captain saw the biggest sperm whale he'd ever seen in his life surfacing not a hundred yards from the ship.

"Look at 'er! Look at the size of 'er!" the lookout shouted, dancing from one foot to the other in excitement.

It took hours to land her, and days to process her properly, but she was the crowning jewel of their trip. The money they received from the sale of the oil made more than one member of the crew a wealthy man indeed, and the captain made sure Nat's widow was well provided for.

For many years afterward, the captain continued sailing his whaleboat out of Nantucket, but he never saw Nat Taylor's ghost again.

21

The Jewelry Box

HOLYOKE

They were only halfway home when Judith took poorly. It was the swaying and bouncing of the carriage that did it. She was expecting their first child and had been quite ill for the past few months. Even now, the least little thing set her off.

Richard eyed his pretty young wife with concern, noting the greenish cast to her skin and the tightness of her mouth. He was going to have to find someplace for them to stop for the night. It was already dusk, and the chill of the late autumn wind was seeping into the buggy. They couldn't spend the night here; they would freeze. He began keeping an eye out for an inn or a house. They were on an empty stretch of road, and he had almost despaired of finding something suitable when he saw a light flickering between the trees.

"We're almost there, sweetheart," he told his ailing wife, who nodded wearily and concentrated on keeping her dinner down.

Richard turned the horses down a small farm lane and up a hill. At the peak stood a quaint old house with a small tower on one side and a cupola on the roof. A little old man and his wife appeared at the door, calling out greetings and waving a cheery lantern well before their carriage reached the small front lawn. Within moments Judith was being tenderly escorted into the house by the wife while the husband helped Richard unhitch the carriage and lead the horse to the small stable behind the house.

When they were done, the husband took Richard into the house. He glanced admiringly around the large parlor, which was neat and clean and well-proportioned. Hand-carved chairs were grouped invitingly near the fire, and Judith was lying on the settee holding a steaming drink that smelled of fresh peppermint and herbs. She was looking much better already and was deep in discussion about names for the baby with the pert little wife, who had white curls and twinkling black eyes. The old woman leapt up at once to welcome him with another steaming cup of tea and some gingerbread cookies she'd just pulled out of the oven. Richard was a happy man as he sat down in a carved chair and enjoyed his dessert.

The little old man came in presently, and the two men started talking about carving. Richard carved in his spare time but hoped someday to earn his living making furniture. After he finished his gingerbread, he got up and went to his satchel, which he had deposited in the entryway, and pulled out a dainty mahogany jewelry box that he had carved for his Judith. He brought it into the parlor, and the old man studied it with care. On the far side of the fire, his pert little wife stared and stared at the jewelry box with her twinkling black eyes, a wistful look on her wrinkled face. Richard handed her the box and watched her stroke it lovingly. She gave it back reluctantly, then began clucking over Judith, who was half-asleep on the settee.

The old couple escorted them to their guestroom and bade them goodnight. As they turned to go, Richard awkwardly

THE JEWELRY BOX

mentioned that they would have to make an early start and would probably leave before their hosts arose. He offered to pay them for the night's lodgings, but the old man proudly refused to hear a word of it.

"You are our guests," the old man told them. And that was that.

As they snuggled together under the down quilts, Judith murmured: "Let's leave the jewelry box for them. It would make a nice thank-you gift, and you can always make me another."

Remembering the wistful look on the old woman's face as she stroked the lid, Richard agreed.

The young couple were up before dawn the next morning, and Judith was a new woman after the herbal remedy and the rest. They tiptoed downstairs, and Richard carefully removed the jewelry box from his satchel and placed it on a prominent place on the mantle above the parlor fireplace. They snuck out to the barn, hitched the horse to the buggy, and soon were driving down the steep lane toward the road. Something nagged at the back of Richard's mind the whole way down the drive, and when they reach the bottom, he realized what it was. He'd heard a clanging sound when he took the jewelry box out of the satchel, as if one of his carving knives had dropped onto the floor. Chagrined, he stopped the horse and checked his satchel. And he was right. His favorite knife was no longer there.

"I'll have to run back and get it," he told Judith. "It costs too much to replace easily."

She nodded and watched as he slipped down from the seat and trotted back up the hill. He quickly reached the top, panting a little after the steep climb, and then stopped short in amazement. Before him was a weedy, overgrown lawn overlooked by a decrepit old house with rotting boards, a caved-in roof, a sagging front porch, and broken windows. The tower was completely covered with vines so that only a few gaps showed here and there. It had obviously not housed anyone for many years and couldn't possibly be the place they had stayed last night. Yet there was no other house for miles around.

Richard didn't know how long he stood gazing in shock at the ruins of the house. After a long, long time, he heard footsteps behind him, and Judith's voice called: "Richard, is everything all right? Did you find the carving knife?"

Then she was at his side and stopped as suddenly as he. "Richard!" she gasped. "This can't be the house!" But it was.

Comforted by his wife's presence, Richard found the courage to venture closer to the ruined home. Judith dogged his heels. Together they peered through one of the broken windows into what remained of the front parlor. And then Judith gasped and pointed toward the fireplace. Standing in the center of the mantle was the carved jewelry box. And gleaming beside it lay Richard's best carving knife.

22

Dark Portrait

BOSTON

He had violently hated the portrait from the moment he first stepped foot in Province House. The governor had it hanging in his library, and whenever Hutchinson's duties took him there, the lieutenant governor kept his back to the painting to avoid seeing the twisted, sour visage of the man represented therein. The portrait's eyes seemed to watch him as he moved restlessly about the governor's library, and he hated meeting that dark gaze.

The governor saw him staring at it one day and told him about the man it portrayed. It was a painting of Edward Randolph, the English loyalist. Randolph was an English colonial agent who attacked the legality of the Massachusetts Bay charter and helped bring about the withdrawal of New Hampshire from the colony's administration. Randolph was disliked by the settlers because he believed that the colony should repeal all laws unfavorable to England and because he enforced the hated Navigation Acts. When Randolph moved to Boston to become collector of customs for New England, his relations with the colonials were extremely bitter. The portrait of the man was painted around this time, and the colonists believed that it was infected by the foul, evil spirit of the man who stood against everything they believed in. Seeing the dark visage portrayed on the canvas, Hutchinson could understand how that rumor had gotten started.

The lieutenant governor privately decided that he would not have liked Randolph, though he approved of his loyalty to England. It disturbed him that such a dark portrait had been hung in such a prominent place. But it was not for him to determine what decorations were in Province House, and so he said nothing.

As he rode home in the carriage after this latest meeting, Hutchinson kept seeing the portrait in his mind. So he forced himself to think instead about the new Stamp Act imposed on the Colony by the British. The Stamp Act was passed by the British Parliament on March 22, 1765. The new tax was imposed on all American colonists and required them to pay a tax on every piece of printed paper, including ship's papers, legal documents, licenses, newspapers, and even playing cards. Hutchinson did not approve of the new law and had spoken his mind to the governor about it.

In the past, taxes and duties on colonial trade had been meant to regulate commerce. But the Stamp Act was different. England was using the new tax to raise money to pay for the French and Indian War, and it was passed without the approval of the colonial legislatures. They were being taxed without legal representation in the British Parliament, and this had caused an uproar.

Still, Hutchinson was loyal to the Crown and would follow its laws, even if he disagreed with them. But there would be trouble over this. He knew it in his bones. For some reason, the vision of the dark portrait rose before his eyes at this thought, and he shuddered, pulled his cloak close about him, and hurried into his house.

Resentment grew over the new taxation, not just in Massachusetts but throughout the colonies. Soon citizens were protesting in the streets. In August, Andrew Oliver, distributor of stamps for Massachusetts, was hung in effigy from a giant elm tree in the city's South End. Hutchinson immediately ordered the sheriff to remove the offensive object, but a large crowd opposed the sheriff, and he had to back down. Later the crowd marched the effigy through the streets, where they tore down the real Oliver's office and ransacked his home at the foot of Fort Hill, beheading and burning the effigy along with Oliver's stable house and coach and chaise. The sheriff and lieutenant governor were stoned when they tried to stop the mob, which then proceeded to loot and destroy the contents of Oliver's house.

A few days later, Hutchinson woke in the middle of the night, shaking from head to toe from a terrible nightmare in which Randolph—the man in the dark portrait—entered his room and hung over his bed, reaching toward him with claw-like hands. He lay awake until dawn, afraid to fall asleep lest he see that dark face looming over him again.

Hutchinson was dining with his family the evening of August 15 when fists began pounding on the door, and angry voices demanded that he come out. He saw at once that an out-of-control mob had arrived at his house. He quickly gathered up his family and fled while the mob gutted his home, tearing down walls, smashing windows, emptying the wine cellar, and—worst of all to his mind—ransacking his library and hurling invaluable manuscripts about the Massachusetts province, which he had been thirty years in collecting, into the mud. Clinging to his sobbing family, the lieutenant governor saw again in his mind the warning face of the man in the dark portrait and shuddered.

It was hard to pick up the pieces, but Hutchinson rebuilt his home, comforted his family, and kept doing his duty with a dogged determination, despite the grumbling of the colonists. Four years had thus passed when the governor suddenly resigned, and Hutchinson found himself elevated to the role of acting governor and moved with his family into Province House.

As he stood in the main hallway of the house, watching his belongings being carried in, Hutchinson tried to ignore the knowledge that he was now living with the strange portrait that sent shivers up his spine whenever he entered his new library.

"Take it down or cover it up," his daughter said to her father one morning after she had passed shuddering underneath the spooky portrait with its bitter, living eyes and sour face. Feeling relieved, the acting governor ordered curtains to be hung around the dark portrait, and he kept them closed; ostensibly to please his daughter, but in reality to please himself. Still, he could feel its presence whenever he sat in the meeting room, as if the evil eyes were yet watching him through the curtain.

For some reason, the dark face in the portrait began haunting his dreams in the winter of 1770. Again and again, he would see the face of Edward Randolph looming over him with an evil smile that made his flesh creep. After one such dream, he woke screaming so loud that he brought the servants running into his bedroom to see what was wrong. His doctor insisted that the dreams were caused by all the stress he was under and made him take a few days off to rest.

The doctor was right about the stress. It was a difficult time for the acting governor. Conflicts between the British and the colonists had been on the rise as the British government attempted to increase its control over the colonies. The troops brought in by the former governor back in 1768 were considered a thorn in the side of the common folk, and they acted as a constant reminder of the increase in taxes forced upon colonists. The townspeople and the soldiers had had numerous conflicts throughout the city, and each new report tied another knot into the acting governor's stomach.

Hutchinson was sitting in the study writing on a wintry evening in early March when a cold breeze swept suddenly through the room, chilling him to the bone. Hutchinson turned quickly toward the window, wondering why the servants had opened it. But it was closed. The icy wind swept around him once more, and suddenly the curtains surrounding the dark portrait burst apart. Before his eyes, the dark figure of Edward Randolph stepped forth from the frame and hovered halfway between floor and ceiling.

Hutchinson gasped and stumbled out of his chair in a sudden panic. The glowing figure reached toward him with gnarled hands that seemed to the stunned man as if they were claws. And then the door burst open behind the acting governor, bringing in the warmth and bustle of the hallway and the frantic face of one of his men.

"Come quickly, sir," he gasped, panting heavily from his run. "The soldiers have opened fire on the crowd. I think some of the townsmen are dead!"

As they rushed toward King Street, the man gasped out the tale. The men in the streets had been restless all evening, and several confrontations had occurred between the colonists and the British soldiers. The one in King Street started when an apprentice taunted a British officer, accusing him of not paying his bill for a new wig that he'd bought. A sentry named White who was on duty that night had overheard the apprentice and sprang to the defense of his fellow soldier. A heated exchange followed, and the sentry struck the apprentice with his musket, knocking him to the ground. The ruckus attracted a mob of some fifty men. Alone and outnumbered, White retreated to the Custom House steps, loaded his gun, and waved it about in a panicked attempt to push away the crowd. "Turn out, Main Guard," he yelled from his perch.

In front of the Main Guard, Captain Thomas Preston ordered his men to help support White. Lining up in columns of two, Preston and seven of his solders moved across King Street with fixed bayonets and pushed through the crowd until they reached the beleaguered White. But when Preston tried to march the men back to the Main Guard, the mob began pressing in on them, hurling coal, snowballs, sticks, and oyster shells at the soldiers. Preston ordered the crowd to disperse, but before he could bring some order to the unruly mob, a large club-wielding man grabbed one of his soldier's bayonets and knocked him to the ground. The soldier—a man named Montgomery—leapt to his feet, shouting, "Damn you, fire!" and unloaded his musket in the direction of the crowd.

Upon hearing the word "fire," several other soldiers also began firing into the crowd. In a matter of minutes, five civilians lay dying in the streets; another half dozen lay injured.

The soldiers were reloading their weapons and preparing to

fire again when Captain Preston recovered his wits enough to yell, "Stop firing! Do not fire!"

Hutchinson's mind was racing as he listened to the tale. A disaster of this magnitude would have far-reaching consequences, and he was furious that the soldiers had allowed this to happen. When he reached King Street, he pushed his way over to Captain Preston, shouting: "Do you know, Sir, you have no power to fire on any body of the public collected together except you have a civil magistrate with you give orders?"

After talking with Preston, Hutchinson hurried into the Town House, where several members of the Council had already gathered. Assuring the gathered Council members that he would see justice done, Hutchinson stepped out onto a balcony overlooking the scene of the massacre and asked the crowd for calm. "Let the law have its course," he called down to them. "I will live and die by the law."

Preston and eight soldiers were arrested later that night. The event was dubbed the Boston Massacre by the colonists and used as colonial propaganda against the British. A week after the incident, a grand jury handed down indictments against Captain Preston and eight soldiers.

The next few months were some of the most difficult that the acting governor had ever faced. Many prominent Boston residents, including such notable figures as Samuel Adams and John Hancock, demanded the instant removal of all troops from the city. Hutchinson balked at taking such an action but was finally forced to give in to overwhelming public pressure. The two regiments evacuated the city and moved to Castle William. Hutchinson stood firm, however, against the demand for a quick trial of the soldiers, determined to give tempers time to cool.

The British soldiers were brought to trial in the fall of 1770. Captain Preston was defended by Attorney John Adams, who would later become president of the United States. After a lengthy trial, Preston was acquitted of the charges against him. The other soldiers involved in the incident were defended at a second trial. After less than three hours of deliberation, the jury acquitted six of the soldiers on all charges. The other two soldiers were found guilty of manslaughter.

The trial could not be over too soon for the acting governor, and when the final verdicts were reported, Hutchinson sagged with relief. But although this ordeal had ended, the province remained a hotbed of unrest, and Samuel Adams was a constant thorn in his side, opposing him at every turn. Nonetheless, Hutchinson persisted in supporting the Crown, even though he deplored the methods it employed, and in 1771, a formal decree naming Hutchinson Royal Governor of the Massachusetts Bay Province was handed down.

Then, in 1772, the British Parliament passed a special act strengthening the powers of the royal governors in America. The act provided for the payment of the salaries of the governors and judges independent of the colonial assemblies. Hutchinson was delighted, but the assembly was not. Stupid of him not to realize how the assemblymen would react, he saw in hindsight. The assembly denounced the act as a violation of its charter and called it a bribe—a bribe used by the Crown to ensure the faithfulness of the royal governors and to encourage them to stand against colonial rights. The subject was taken up at a town meeting in Boston, and a large committee was appointed to draw up and publish a statement of all the grievances of the colonies. The address was prepared by Samuel Adams and Joseph

Warren, and Hutchinson considered it the most seditious and treasonable address he had ever heard. His was not a popular response, and it further aroused the indignation of the people against the new governor.

Hutchinson found himself retreating as often as he could to his study, trying to find some peace and quiet in a world that was anything but. He was reading some letters by the fire in his study one evening when a soft whisper of wind blew across his cheek. He knew from the prickling sensation on his neck that he was no longer alone in the room, and he slowly turned his head to look toward the dark portrait of Randolph. He had been meaning to have it removed from the library after the night of the massacre, but political events had swept it from his mind. The ghost of Randolph was standing behind his chair, glaring at him. Hutchinson stared back, hands shaking. For a long moment man and ghost stared at one another. Then Randolph was gone. The governor collapsed into his chair, wondering why the ghost had reappeared to him at this moment. He was soon to learn.

The very next day he discovered, to his horror, that letters he and other colony leaders had written to one of the undersecretaries of the English government had been put into the hands of Dr. Benjamin Franklin, who had procured them by stratagem from the office where they were stored. In these letters, Hutchinson had vilified the popular leaders of Massachusetts, had condemned the liberal clauses of the Massachusetts charter, and had recommended the punishment of the Bostonians by restraints upon both their rights as British citizens and their commercial privileges. Benjamin Franklin believed that the letters proved Hutchinson and his fellow leaders to be conspiring against the colonists. He sent them to the speaker of the Massachusetts assembly, who had them read aloud before the assembly and then published for everyone in the colony to read.

Hutchinson was appalled to find his private thoughts brought to light in such a fashion. Thinking the letters confidential, he had freely expressed his true opinions about certain popular leaders of Massachusetts and urged strong measures against the citizens of Boston. Remembering the look on the face of Edward Randolph as the ghost stood behind his chair, Hutchinson knew this situation would not end well. And he was right. The tempest of indignation that followed these revelations was fateful to Hutchinson.

A committee was appointed to wait upon the governor and demand from him an explicit denial or acknowledgment of their authenticity. "They are mine," Hutchinson said, "but they were quite confidential." Following this confirmation of the authenticity of the letters, the assembly adopted a petition to the king asking for the removal of Hutchinson and his lieutenant, calling them public slanderers and enemies of the colony.

For Hutchinson, the nightmare of his days was compounded now by the nightmare of his nights. He was haunted by the memory of the portrait coming to life in his study, and the cruel Edward Randolph now came to him almost every night in his dreams until he could hardly sleep for the dread of it.

Meanwhile, the governor still had duties to perform—however meaningless they seemed to the people of his province—and so he did them. One of these duties was to approve the docking of three East India Company ships loaded with tea in Boston Harbor. This was a controversial act that earned

Hutchinson yet more censure, for the East India Company—in cahoots with the British parliament—was attempting to export half a million pounds of tea to the colonies without paying the usual duties and tariffs, thus underselling American merchants and monopolizing the tea trade. Such unfair commerce practices revived the colonists' passions about the issue of taxation without representation. The East India ships landed on November 27, 1773, but were prevented from unloading their cargo. Demanding that the East India Company return the tea to whence it came or face retribution, the Sons of Liberty, led by Samuel Adams, began holding regular meetings to determine the fate of the three cargo ships in the Boston harbor.

Things had completely spiraled out of Hutchinson's control, but he kept up appearances, although he was haggard and worn from his sleepless, nightmare-filled nights and stressful days. His family worried about him constantly, but what could he do? He had a job to perform, no matter how distasteful it might be.

Hutchinson was standing at his library window at dusk on December 16, 1773, when a chill wind bit into the back of his neck and he heard the curtains around the portrait of Edward Randolph flapping wildly. Hutchinson turned slowly, stiffly, as if he had suddenly realized that he was an old man, and looked toward the dark portrait. The figure of Edward Randolph was hovering halfway between floor and ceiling, shining with a fierce black light, his eyes blazing with orange-white fire. Most incongruously, he held a steaming cup of tea in his hand. Hutchinson stared at the phantom without expression. After the nightmare of the past year, a mere ghost no longer had power to stir him.

The two men stared at one another for a tense moment and then the ghost smashed the teacup on the stone hearth of

DARK PORTRAIT

the fireplace and vanished. For a moment, pieces of shattered porcelain gleamed against the stone; then they too vanished. All save one. Hutchinson bent down to pick it up. It had a sharp edge that nicked his finger, and a single drop of blood welled up. Hutchinson stared at it dully. The Sons of Liberty were meeting about the tea ships again today. Something controversial would come of it, Hutchison thought. That much was apparent from Randolph's visit. Hutchinson sank into an armchair and stared into the flames of the fire, their warmth failing to penetrate the chill of his body, waiting for the bad news that he was sure would come soon.

At the same instant the phantom appeared to Hutchinson, a large band of patriots disguised as Mohawk Indians burst from the South Meeting House. The patriots headed toward Griffin's Wharf, where the tea ships were moored, watched by a silent crowd of sympathizers. The Sons of Liberty boarded each of the ships and went to work, striking chests of tea with axes and hatchets. Once the crates were opened, the patriots dumped the tea into the sea. By nine o'clock, the Sons of Liberty had emptied a total of 342 crates of tea into Boston Harbor. When they were through, the patriots marched off the wharf, tomahawks and axes resting on their shoulders, and a fife played as they marched past the home where the British admiral stood spying on their work. As they passed, the admiral called: "Well, boys, you've had a pleasant evening for your Indian caper, haven't you? But mind, you've yet to pay the fiddler!"

Hutchinson stood silent and still when the report was brought to him. His apathy unnerved the man who brought him the message, who noticed with a shudder that Hutchison's face looked just like that of the dark portrait hanging above him. When Hutchinson told his family what had happened, he also told him he feared this was the end of his career. And he was right. In April 1774, King George III and the British parliament closed the port of Boston in response to the patriots' "tea party." Four British regiments were sent to Boston, along with a new military governor—General Thomas Gage—who was Hutchinson's replacement.

Hutchinson packed up his family and his belongings and set sail for England, never to return to the country of his birth. As he mounted the ramp onto the ship which would take him away forever, he caught a glimpse of the ghost of Edward Randolph standing silent and still on the dock as sailors and dockhands swirled around and through him. The former governor raised his hand in silent greeting and farewell to the man in the dark portrait who had haunted so many of his days in office. Then Hutchinson stepped onto the deck of the ship and did not look back again.

23

Time Warp

LEXINGTON

I am a Revolutionary War buff, and I jumped at the chance to visit Lexington and Concord while traveling with friends through Massachusetts. I was only sorry that no battle reenactments were scheduled for the weekend of our trip. Still, this was my first visit to the site, and I intended to enjoy every minute of it.

We got caught in a traffic jam on the highway and arrived late into Lexington. I had only a few minutes to stand on the Green and picture the events of April 18 and 19, 1775, in my mind before darkness fell. But I stood as long as I could, imagining the scene as it must have taken place on those fateful days.

Paul Revere, summoned by Dr. Joseph Warren on the night of April 18, was instructed to ride to Lexington and warn Sam Adams and John Hancock that British troops were marching to arrest them. After being rowed across the Charles River by two associates, Paul Revere rode a borrowed horse toward Lexington, stopping at each house along the way to warn them of the approach of the British.

Responding instantly to the news, local leaders summoned the Yankee militia. Drums beat, bells pealed, and men hurried to this very green, where they lined up in battle formation and watched the British redcoats under the command of Major Pitcairn march toward them through the dawn fog.

When the British officer swung his sword and threatened the defiant Yankees, the militia leader ordered his men to disperse. As they retreated, a shot rang out, and the British retaliated, firing upon the retreating militia, killing eight and wounding ten more.

After this confrontation, the British soldiers advanced to Concord to seek and destroy military supplies and ammunition stored there by the colonists. They encountered a group of armed militia at Concord's North Bridge. This time, when threatened, the Americans fought back.

The Americans routed the British, who retreated first to Concord center and then toward Boston. By then, militia and minutemen from all surrounding towns were on the move, and they used small squad tactics to flank the British column and shoot at the soldiers from behind walls and trees, inflicting heavy damage. The redcoats had little experience with such tactics, and their morale was quickly destroyed. The British relief brigade under Lord Percy came to their rescue, using two cannon to disperse the provincials and collecting the troops back into regiments. But by the time the British soldiers made it back to Boston, they had suffered nearly 20 percent casualties.

The actions of April 19 led to the siege of Boston and the start of the Revolutionary War.

By the time I reached this juncture in my musings, it was fully dark and my friends were impatient. So I tore myself from the Green, promising myself a good look around in the morning, and went to enjoy a good meal at a local restaurant. Then my friends and I headed back to the inn for a good night's rest.

I fell asleep almost immediately, only to snap awake in the middle of the night, sure I had heard the sound of bells ringing. I lay listening for a long time but heard nothing more than the wind in the trees outside the inn. Unable to fall back asleep, I rose and went to the window. The moon was full, and the night glimmered with dancing, silvery lights and flickering shadows. I found myself drawn outside, as if summoned by a voice calling my name. I dressed quickly and hurried outdoors.

I emerged through the lobby doors into darkness and blinked, wondering where the silvery moonlight had gone. Before I could recover my wits, a hand appeared out of nowhere and yanked me into the bushes.

"Wh . . . what?" I spluttered and found myself face to face with a young lad wearing a baggy Minuteman uniform two sizes too big for him. He'd put his cocked hat on backward in his excitement, and I could see his dark eyes sparkling in the dim light.

"There you are," he said. "Where have you been? Didn't you hear the alarm bells? Revere rode through just now. The British are coming! Captain's called together the Minutemen. We're to gather on the Green. Come on."

He jerked about and ran off. I gaped after him for a moment and then started to grin. This was obviously a reenactment of the events of 1775. And what an incredible reenactment it was! That young fellow was good! He even smelled the part—having obviously not bathed properly in at least a week.

"Hurry up," he called over his shoulder. "We've got to arm ourselves. Unless you want to face the redcoats without a musket?"

"Not me," I replied, gesturing emphatically with my hand. I blinked a little, noticing that I too appeared to be in colonial dress. Strange. I didn't remember putting on a costume. I shrugged off the quiver of fear that ran up my spine and gave myself over to this strange, nighttime reenactment.

I followed my guide through trees and bushes and bracken. I didn't remember this much shrubbery from my afternoon stroll around town, nor did I remember the dirt road we shortly found ourselves on. As we drew closer to town, we saw people milling about everywhere we looked, exclaiming and planning and arming up. Bells were ringing, drums were banging. More and more men were arriving in their makeshift militia uniforms. It was a madhouse!

A few minutes of dodging and weaving through the crowd got us to the meetinghouse where the magazine was stored. Several older fellows made sure we had muskets. One of the men twirled the young lad's hat to face forward and smartened him up a bit. I was given an approving nod by the same man, and then we were sent to Buckman's tavern, where some of the other Minutemen were awaiting further orders. Speculation was rife among the rowdy lot. Some believed that the redcoats were approaching; others thought it was just hysteria.

I wrinkled my nose and downed a pint of ale, grimacing at the smell of all those unwashed bodies jammed together in the bar. These fellows were good. I could almost swear I was really back in 1775. The streets were dirty and full of horse-droppings (I wasn't sure how they'd managed that), the dialect these fellows spoke was hard to follow, and my young companion was going on and on about some girl he hoped to impress with his exploits as a soldier. Very lifelike.

Then we heard the sharp rat-a-tat of the drum, calling us to the Green. Captain Parker had received word that the

British were half a mile away. Dawn was approaching as Parker led about forty of us to the north end of Lexington Common, near the Bedford Road, and formed us in a single file. I was stationed in the center of the company. The men around me stank of sweat and fear. Most of them didn't appear to believe that the British would fire on us, until a few of the men mentioned the way the redcoats had fired upon civilians in the Boston Massacre. After that, we stood grave and silent, waiting.

The sky was turning gray with the approach of dawn, though the landscape was muffled by a heavy fog. It was too easy to imagine ghosts in that fog, and I shivered, amazed at how realistic this nighttime reenactment was, down to the swirling fog and the tense bodies around me. We could hear the sound of marching footsteps approaching down the road. Slowly, redcoats appeared through the mist.

I heard Captain Parker say, "Stand your ground. Don't fire unless fired upon." Drawing a deep breath, he added, "But if they want a war, let it begin here."

The British troops approached us rapidly in platoons, with an officer on horseback at their head. The officer halted his men, then swung his sword, saying, "Lay down your arms, rebels, or you are all dead men!"

I gaped up at him through the foggy dawn as a chill ran down my spine. His face was grim and lined, his accent flawless, and in that moment I would have sworn on a stack of Bibles that these events were real.

I heard Parker call us to disperse, then heard a shot fired. Immediately, the British raised their guns, and I wanted to throw myself to the ground and scramble for cover. Which was

TIME WARP

nonsense, of course. The guns were only charged with powder. Weren't they?

For a timeless heartbeat, I stared down the muzzle of the British guns. Then shots rang out so loudly they hurt my ears, and all about me was a confusion of smoke and flash and fog and the groans of the dying.

Suddenly the world went dark—just as it had when I had left the inn. When my vision cleared, I realized that everyone had vanished, and I was standing alone on the Green in the bright moonlight, my ears still ringing with the sound of gunfire. I scanned the Green frantically, looking for the reenactors, but no one was there. That's when I realized that it hadn't been a reenactment. It had been real. I had stepped out the door of the inn and had gone back in time.

The thought terrified me, and I ran all the way back to the inn, threw myself into bed fully clothed, and spent the rest of the night with my head under the covers, trying to tell myself it was all a dream. But I knew it wasn't.

My friends were surprised at my subdued behavior the next day as we explored Lexington and Concord. The historical exhibits and the monuments would have delighted me any other time, but after experiencing the real deal the night before, I must confess that they left me feeling a little flat. But how could I explain this? I couldn't. They'd think me mad. So I forced myself to appear enthusiastic and went through the motions as best I could.

In the back of my mind, I kept replaying the night's events. It must have been a time warp, I thought. There was no other way to explain it. I had no history of sleepwalking and had never heard of a dream that included smells and sounds like those I'd experienced last night on the Green. But how had it happened? And why? I'd probably never know.

As we packed ourselves into the car for the long drive home, I realized I was glad I had come. To reenact history was one thing. To live it—no matter how uncomfortably—was another. I'd been given a rare gift, and perhaps someday I would be able to share the story with someone who would believe me. Perhaps.

24

Elixir of Life

MALDEN

I suppose I shouldn't have told the story to my friend. I should have known what his reaction would be. But tell it I did. After all, he was attending the medical school at Harvard, and what brand-new doctor wouldn't be interested in a local story about the elixir of life? I didn't think he'd take it seriously!

Anyway, the tale was a short one, but intriguing. A rich but reclusive resident of my town named Gray had lived alone in a big house with one manservant to care for his needs. He was a rude, sullen sort of fellow with a sour, twisted face that I daresay not even a mother would love. Gray could be seen at night, working in his room on some sort of mysterious experiment, but he would tell no one what he was up to, and he was so angry and unpleasant when casual inquiries were made that folks soon ceased talking to him at all.

About twenty years ago, now, Gray took sick and passed away quite suddenly. His manservant lived alone in the mansion, then, heir to the man's entire fortune—but with one caveat: The servant had to make sure that nothing whatsoever was done to Gray's body before burial. This perplexed the local mortician, who sourly inquired why he was not allowed to perform the usual embalming process on the miser's body. The servant's reply? That his master had spent all his mortal days trying to develop a chemical formula for the elixir of life.

According to the servant, Gray had come very close indeed to finding an elixir that would prolong life indefinitely, if not forever. But a sudden, fatal illness had come upon him before he could complete the formula. However, the miser believed that his life's work had not been in vain. He told his servant that the formula was already so well developed that it would act as a preservative of the flesh, and that Gray's dead body would not decay in the years to come. His final request was that his body be interred as is. In doing thus, the manservant might be able to check on Gray's corpse in a year or two to see if the secret elixir had indeed worked as predicted. If so, the servant could sell the elixir as a replacement for the embalming products currently on the market and thus become a rich man.

The mortician grumbled at such a strange request but acceded to the wishes of the deceased. Gray's untouched body was placed in a vault at the local cemetery, and the manservant settled down to wait and see if the elixir truly worked as predicted. Unfortunately for him, he too was stricken with a sudden illness that took his life soon afterward, and with him died the secret formula for the elixir of life.

My friend listened intently as I related the story, and then asked: "So what happened when they opened the vault?"

"Opened the vault?" I repeated stupidly. "What do you mean, opened the vault?"

My almost-a-doctor friend straightened in surprise. "You mean no one ever went back to check?"

I stared at him with my jaw open in shock. I snapped it shut.

"Of course not," I said, narrowing my eyes. I knew what was coming. I could see it in his eyes.

"Well, let's go take a look," he said, as predicted. His pals all nodded eagerly. Medical students are all alike, I thought grimly. I argued against it during the carriage ride to Malden, and all the way to the graveyard. No one paid any attention to me, except to ask me directions to the crypt.

I stayed stubbornly outside while they pried open the door and went in to look.

My friend appeared suddenly at the door. "You've got to see this," he said, his face aglow in the lantern light. He pulled me inside, and a moment later I was staring down at an almost perfectly preserved corpse. "I'm not sure he would have appreciated the browning effect," I remarked after fighting with my churning stomach for a moment. "And he's slightly withered around the edges."

"Nonsense. Just a little wear and tear. Considering he's been twenty years in the grave, this is marvelous preservation. We've got to get our hands on that elixir."

His almost-doctor buddies nodded vigorously, shadows of their bobbing heads reflecting on the walls of the crypt. I was seriously spooked by the scene, and most of all by the corpse at my feet. "The secret of the formula died with the old manservant," I reminded my friend.

"But it is still there, inside his skin," pointed out a red-haired young fellow with a pimply face, to whom I took an instant dislike. The chap's blue eyes sparkled in the dim light of the lantern, but a flickering shadow hid his mouth and chin so I couldn't read his expression.

ELIXIR OF LIFE

"What are you going to do, take a sample?" I asked sarcastically.

"I think we should take the whole head," the red-haired chap said calmly. This was too much for me.

"I won't be a party to it," I said, glaring at my friend and whirling away. From the corner of my eye, I saw my friend shrug philosophically at his doctor-buddies, and then they bent over the corpse and started discussing the best way to remove its head. I went outside and sat down in the shrubbery to wait.

I was half asleep, leaning against a small bush, when a dreadful moan startled me into wakefulness. Pulse pounding in wrist and throat, I leapt to my feet as the horrible moan came again, followed by phantom footsteps. A moment later, my friend and his doctor-buddies came hurtling out of the crypt clutching several lanterns and a severed head.

"Close it! Close it!" shouted my friend. The young men pushed against the door, and a moment later it slammed shut with a loud bang, cutting off the deep moaning. I was shaking so much I could barely stand, and my body was pulsing from hot to cold as I watched my fellow students sealing the door as best they could.

"Let's get out of here," my friend said, echoing the sentiment of us all. We raced out of the cemetery and leapt into the carriage, setting off for Harvard at a breakneck pace. I stared once or twice in disapproval at the head that had been muffled in a cloak and thrust into the corner, but I said nothing. None of us wished to return to that haunted place, even to take back the head. Remembering the horrible moaning, my hands twitched in my lap, turning cold as ice. I tucked them under my arms and was very glad when my friend dropped me off at my rooms.

I tried to put the incident out of my mind over the next

several weeks as I studied for my exams. When I had passed them successfully, I headed home to Malden to stay with my parents over the holidays. It was at dinner my first night home that my mother mentioned a rumor that was going around town. Apparently, some folks claimed to have seen a withered, headless corpse stalking around the town cemetery from midnight to dawn. It appeared to be searching for something. I choked, tried to swallow the mouthful of milk I'd just drunk, and spent the next ten minutes coughing and gasping. By the time I'd recovered my breath, my parents had forgotten the topic of conversation in their concern for me. But I hadn't.

I spent the rest of the evening worrying over my mother's comment. What had we done? Was Gray's corpse haunting the local cemetery, or was it just a false rumor? I absolutely did not want to know. I told myself this again and again as I lay awake under the quilts on my bed. I told myself this as I slipped into my clothes, pulled a jacket tightly about me, slid through my bedroom window, and climbed down the pine tree outside. I kept repeating it as my eyes adjusted to the bright moonlight and my footsteps thudded gently along the road to the cemetery. And I repeated it as I approached the crypt, wanting to flee almost as much as I wanted to see what would happen.

I found the bush where I had crouched so many months ago and settled myself down to wait in the cold, thankful that no snow had fallen yet this season. It was a nice night. The stars were twinkling; the moon was full; the air was crisp. Nothing was going to happen, I decided, stretching sleepily. It was complete nonsense.

That was when the banging started. Thud! Thud! Thud! Horrible, huge sounds came from the crypt in front of me. On the final thud, the iron door blew open with a mighty crash, and I cowered backward as icy waves of foul air flowed forth, stinging my nose and roiling my stomach. A withered figure in mildewed clothes emerged from the gaping mouth of the crypt, groping its way forward. It had no head atop the ragged brown skin of its neck. The moonlight struck cruelly down upon the figure as it stalked forward into the cemetery.

I gave a shout of sheer terror and leapt to my feet. I ran, leaping gravestones and dodging bushes, trees, and massive Christmas floral arrangements left before prominent tombs. The withered, headless figure seemed to be following in my footsteps, which made me run even faster. In moments I was out of the graveyard and fleeing for home. I swarmed up the pine tree, dove through the window, and a moment later was crouched underneath my bed. I lay shuddering and gasping for nearly an hour before I recovered enough to shut my window against the cold night air and crawl under the covers.

I never went near the cemetery again and told no one about my nighttime exploits. Word eventually got around about the medical students' caper and its grisly aftermath, but no one in town associated the story with me, for which I was grateful. Apparently, Gray's withered corpse wandered the cemetery for many years in search of its head, which was never returned. The cemetery was eventually relocated, and the tomb with its headless owner was buried forever, which put an end to the wanderings of the corpse.

My friend never discovered the secret elixir of life, though he experimented with the withered head for many years. Perhaps it was best that way. Some things should remain unknown.

25

The Devil's Altar

PITTSFIELD

He was hunting alone through the Berkshire Hills on that fateful day. It had been a successful hunt, and by late afternoon he was stomping toward home with a large buck strapped to his shoulders. He hesitated for a long moment before taking the fork in the trail that would lead him through Wizard's Glen. It was a deep, narrow valley with strange echoes that did not always repeat back the words that you had spoken. The stories that were told about the place spoke of blood and demons and human sacrifice. Everyone he knew avoided the valley, and he was of a mind to do the same. Except that it was the quickest way home, and the afternoon was already far gone. So he took the left fork and hoped the stories were just that . . . stories.

He was only partway through the valley and had just passed the red-brown stone that many called the Devil's Altar when he heard the first booming-crash of thunder and saw the world darkening around him. The storm moved into the valley with supernatural speed, and he found himself breaking into a run, hoping to find the cave that the boys in the village used when they snuck out to the valley on one of their daredevil larks. He'd heard them discussing it with his young son more than once when they thought he was safely out of earshot.

He stumbled under his heavy burden but refused to leave his hard-won deer behind. He banged his shin against a tree stump, cursed, nearly fell, regained his balance, and then saw the cavern entrance not far from the Devil's Altar. He leapt inside, though not before the first sheets of heavy rain had soaked him to the skin. Panting, he flung himself and his burden on the floor, landing painfully on top of the pocket Bible he kept in his jacket. He shifted off the holy book with a grimace and then tried to squeeze some of the water out of his coat. The cold that accompanied the storm made his teeth chatter. And the ferocity of the thunder and wind amazed him. The rain pounded the earth as if it wanted to kill it, and the wind seemed to howl with devilish overtones. Almost, he thought he could hear voices in the wind. Then he realized he *was* hearing the horrid, shrieking voices of many demons chanting in a language he did not wish to know. It made his hair stand on end.

Abandoning his deer, he crawled quietly toward the entrance of the cave, staying low, and gazed outside into the storm. Before him, mysterious flames had sprung from the ground in two long rows, outlining a road from valley's end to the Devil's Altar. The flames burned so hot that the driving rain evaporated before it could quench the fires. He could see movement at the far end of the long aisle. After a moment of unbelieving study, he realized that it was caused by hundreds of swirling, capering forms dancing their way toward the altar. Horns, tails, bat wings, twisted faces, scales, stingers, and many other foul features adorned the dancing demons; some seemed creatures of flesh and blood, while others seemed to be made of little more than mist and fire and smoke. The smoke-beings swirled in and about the other creatures, half-obscuring them. The demons all reveled in the flashing lightning, the roaring thunder, and the heavy sheets of rain, waving pitchforks and swords and poles whenever lightning smashed into the soaking ground.

The hunter shuddered and slipped behind a rock just inside the entrance to the cavern. This was a festival of demons. And where there were demons . . . He looked over the dancing hoards that were rapidly approaching the Devil's Altar and in a moment saw the one he was looking for. In a small, quiet space at the center of the terrible crowd walked the tall, upright figure of a man wearing a black cloak lined with red satin. His handsome face was proud and cold as stone. His short hair was guinea-gold, and his dark eyes held no pity or mercy but instead took delight in the worst kinds of pain, cruelty, and death.

Just behind the quiet circle trundled a wheeled cage pulled by two man-shaped creatures with the heads of bulls. Inside the cage was a tattered, ragged urchin with fearful dark eyes and long, curly black hair. Her white face and shaking body were visible in the light of the brimstone flames lining the pathway. The hunter drew a deep breath of horror when he realized what her presence at this terrible celebration meant.

As he lay wondering what to do, the hunter saw that the demonic procession had reached the Devil's Altar. The tall blond man leapt easily onto the rock and called to his minions in a language that made red sparks dance behind the hunter's eyes. Twenty warped, demented creatures and twenty more of the amorphous smoke-beings began marching around and around the altar, chanting a foul song that made the hunter's stomach roil.

Then the cold figure atop the red stone gave a signal, and the

THE DEVIL'S ALTAR

two bull-headed men dragged the young girl out of the cage. She struggled desperately, kicking and biting and screaming as she was carried toward the silent figure on the altar. The blond man held a stone knife in one slender-fingered hand, and he watched the girl's struggles with a small smile on his cold lips.

The hunter knew he had to do something. He had to! But what? How could he take on the demon hoard all alone? The girl gave a soft cry of terror as she was thrown at the Devil's feet and tied down with vines pulled from the surrounding trees. The cry decided him. It sounded so much like the lost whimper his young son had given when the hunter told him that his wife—the lad's mother—had died of consumption.

The hunter leapt from his hiding place, his hand groping for the only thing that might work—the pocket-sized Bible he carried everywhere with him. Holding the holy book high above his head, he shouted: "In the name of God, I command you to stop this evil ceremony!" There came an outraged cry from the demon hoard when they heard the name of God spoken aloud among them. For a moment, the hunter found himself staring deep into the cold black eyes of the blond man atop the altar. Trembling from head to toe, the hunter began saying the Lord's Prayer aloud. Demonic figures stumbled away from him, clapping hands to their ears. The cold figure on top of the stone glared. If eyes alone could annihilate the soul, the hunter would have been past reclaiming. But after a moment, the blond man broke his stare and threw back his head and howled—an alien sound akin to the howl of a wolf. Many voices took up the shriek until it rebounded and echoed through the Wizard's Glen, making the hunter shudder and stumble backward in fear. In the next moment, they were gone—vanished without a trace—leaving the rain-soaked hunter still holding the Bible in front of him, and the terrified girl still bound to the rock.

With a gasp of relief, the hunter slid the Bible back into his jacket and ran forward to release the girl from her bonds. Around them, the storm waned and stopped, no longer fed by the horrible hoard from the netherworld. Gathering up his deer and tenderly helping the girl, the hunter made his way home.

The hunter soon learned that the girl was an indentured servant who had run away from a cruel master. She had been captured by the demons as a sacrifice for their master when she took shelter for the night in the Wizard's Glen. The hunter placed her in the care of his sister while he made inquiries and paid off her indenture. In the year that followed, the hunter and the girl met often as they went about their duties, and fell deeply in love. So he took her as his wife and as a mother for his little son, and the couple lived happily all their days. But no one in that family has ever returned to the Wizard's Glen, from that day to this.

Resources

Asfar, Daniel. *Ghost Stories of America.* Edmonton, AB: Ghost House Books, 2001.

———. *Ghost Stories of the Civil War.* Edmonton, AB: Ghost House Books, 2001.

———. *Haunted Battlefields.* Edmonton, AB: Ghost House Books, 2004.

Battle, Kemp P. *Great American Folklore.* New York: Doubleday & Company, Inc., 1986.

Botkin, B. A., ed. *A Treasury of American Folklore.* New York: Crown, 1944.

———. *A Treasury of New England Folklore.* New York: Crown Publishers, Inc., 1965.

Brewer, J. Mason. *American Negro Folklore.* Chicago: Quadrangle Books, 1972.

Brunvand, Jan Harold. *The Choking Doberman and Other Urban Legends.* New York: W. W. Norton, 1984.

———. *The Vanishing Hitchhiker.* New York: W. W. Norton, 1981.

Cahill, Robert Ellis. *Haunted Ships of the North Atlantic.* Danvers, MA: Old Saltbox Publishing & Distributing, 1997.

———. *Lighthouse Mysteries of the North Atlantic.* Salem, MA: Old Saltbox Publishing, 1998.

———. *New England's Witches and Wizards.* Danvers, MA: Old Saltbox Publishing & Distributing, 1983.

———. *Olde New England's Strange Superstitions.* Danvers, MA: Old Saltbox Publishing & Distributing, 1990.

Citro, Joseph A. *Cursed in New England.* Guilford, CT: Globe Pequot Press, 2004.

———. *Passing Strange*. New York: Houghton Mifflin Co., 1996.

———. *Weird New England*. New York: Sterling Publishing Co., Inc., 2005.

Coffin, Tristram P., and Hennig Cohen, eds. *Folklore in America*. New York: Doubleday & AMP, 1966.

———. *Folklore from the Working Folk of America*. New York: Doubleday, 1973.

Cohen, Daniel. *Ghostly Tales of Love & Revenge*. New York: Putnam Publishing Group, 1992.

Cohen, Daniel, and Susan Cohen. *Hauntings & Horrors*. New York: Dutton Children's Books, 2002.

Coleman, Christopher K. *Ghosts and Haunts of the Civil War*. Nashville, TN: Rutledge Hill Press, 1999.

Cornplanter, J. J. *Legends of the Longhouse*. Philadelphia: J. B. Lippincott, 1938.

Dorson, R. M. *America in Legend*. New York: Pantheon Books, 1973.

Downer, Deborah L. *Classic American Ghost Stories*. Little Rock, AR: August House Publishers, Inc.

Drake, Samuel Adams. *A Book of New England Legends and Folk Lore*. Rutland, VT: Charles E. Tuttle Company, Inc., 1884.

Early, Eleanor. *A New England Sampler*. Boston: Waverly House, 1940.

Editors of Life. *The Life Treasury of American Folklore*. New York: Time Inc., 1961.

Erdoes, Richard, and Alfonso Ortiz. *American Indian Myths and Legends*. New York: Pantheon Books, 1984.

Flanagan, J. T., and A. P. Hudson. *The American Folk Reader*. New York: A. S. Barnes & Co., 1958.

Gordon, Dan, and Joseph, Gary. *Cape Encounters*. Hyannis, MA: Cockle Cover Press, 2004.

Holzer, Hans. *Ghosts of New England*. New York: Wings Books, 1996.

Leach, M. *The Rainbow Book of American Folk Tales and Legends*. New York: The World Publishing Co., 1958.

Leeming, David, and Jake Page. *Myths, Legends, & Folktales of America*. New York: Oxford University Press, 1999.

Macken, Lynda Lee. *Haunted Salem & Beyond*. Forked River, NJ: Black Cat Press, 2001.

McSherry, Frank, Jr., Charles G. Waugh, and Martin H. Greenberg, eds. *New England Ghosts*. Nashville, TN: Rutledge Hill Press, 1990.

Mitchell, Edwin Valentine. *It's an Old New England Custom*. New York: Bonanza Books, Inc., 1946.

Mott, A. S. *Ghost Stories of America*, vol. II. Edmonton, AB: Ghost House Books, 2003.

Nadler, Holly Mascot. *Ghosts of Boston Town*. Camden, ME: Down East Books, 2002.

Norman, Michael, and Beth Scott. *Historic Haunted America*. New York: Tor Books, 1995.

Peck, Catherine, ed. *A Treasury of North American Folk Tales*. New York: W. W. Norton, 1998.

Pitkin, David J. *Ghosts of the Northeast*. New York: Aurora Publications, 2002.

Polley, J., ed. *American Folklore and Legend*. New York: Reader's Digest Association, 1978.

Reevy, Tony. *Ghost Train!* Lynchburg, VA: TLC Publishing, 1998.

Revai, Cheri. *Haunted Massachusetts*. Mechanicsburg, PA: Stackpole Books, 2005.

Roberts, Nancy. *Civil War Ghost Stories & Legends*. Columbia, SC: University of South Carolina Press, 1992.

Schwartz, Alvin. *Scary Stories to Tell in the Dark*. New York: Harper Collins, 1981.

Skinner, Charles M. *American Myths and Legends*, vol. 1. Philadelphia: J. B. Lippincott, 1903.

————. *Myths and Legends of Our Own Land*, vol. 1 & 2. Philadelphia: J. B. Lippincott, 1896.

Spence, Lewis. *North American Indians: Myths and Legends Series*. London: Bracken Books, 1985.

Stevens, Austin N., ed. *Mysterious New England*. Dublin, NH: Yankee, Inc., 1971.

Whittier, John Greenleaf. *Supernaturalism of New England*. Baltimore, MD: Clearfield Company, Inc., 1983.

Zeitlin, Steven J., Amy J. Kotkin, and Holly Cutting Baker. *A Celebration of American Family Folklore*. New York: Pantheon Books, 1982.

About the Author

S. E. Schlosser has been telling stories since she was a
child, when games of "let's
pretend" quickly built themselves into full-length tales
acted out with friends. A
graduate of Houghton Col-
lege, the Institute of Children's Literature, and Rutgers

University, she created and maintains the award-winning Web
site Americanfolklore.net, where she shares a wealth of stories
from all fifty states, some dating back to the origins of America.
Sandy spends much of her time answering questions from visitors to the site. Many of her favorite e-mails come from other
folklorists who delight in practicing the old tradition of who can
tell the tallest tale.

About the Illustrator

Artist Paul Hoffman trained in painting and printmaking, with his first extensive illustration work on assignment in Egypt, drawing ancient wall reliefs for the University of Chicago. His work graces books of many genres—children's titles, textbooks, short story collections, natural history volumes, and numerous cookbooks. For *Spooky Massachusetts,* he employed a scratchboard technique and an active imagination.